Robotics for Young Children

Robotics

for Young Children

STEM Activities and Simple Coding

Ann Gadzikowski

Redleaf Press®
www.redleafpress.org
800-423-8309

Published by Redleaf Press
10 Yorkton Court
St. Paul, MN 55117
www.redleafpress.org

First edition 2018
Cover design by Jim Handrigan
Cover photograph by Monica Kass Rogers
Interior design by Percolator
Typeset in FF Tisa Pro
Interior photography by Monica Kass Rogers and Ann Gadzikowski
Printed in the United States of America
24 23 22 21 20 19 18 17   1 2 3 4 5 6 7 8

Library of Congress Cataloging-in-Publication Data

Names: Gadzikowski, Ann, author.
Title: Robotics for young children : STEM activities and simple coding / Ann Gadzikowski.
Description: First edition. | St. Paul, MN : Redleaf Press, 2017. | Includes bibliographical references.
Identifiers: LCCN 2017023634 (print) | LCCN 2017041119 (ebook) | ISBN 9781605545455 (ebook) |
    ISBN 9781605545448 (paperback)
Subjects: LCSH: Robotics—Study and teaching (Early childhood)—Activity programs. |
    BISAC: EDUCATION / Teaching Methods & Materials / Science & Technology. |
    EDUCATION / Preschool & Kindergarten. | EDUCATION / Teaching Methods & Materials /
    Mathematics. | EDUCATION / Computers & Technology.
Classification: LCC TJ211.26 (ebook) | LCC TJ211.26 .G33 2017 (print) | DDC 372.35/8—dc23
LC record available at https://lccn.loc.gov/2017023634

Printed on acid-free paper

To Beth Dirkes and Leslie Morrison, my crackerjack teammates at the Center for Talent Development, in appreciation for your insights, encouragement, and inspiration

Contents

Chapter 4: How Do Robots Help Us?   113

Chapter 5: How Can We Learn More about Robots?   131

Acknowledgments

I'm grateful to the many educators and experts who have helped me learn about robots and understand the potential of computer science in early childhood education. Many thanks to Frances Judd for first introducing me to the term "tangible tech" and to Brian Puerling for showing me that technology can be a powerful tool for intentional teachers. Thank you to Chip Donohue, Tamara Kaldor, Amanda Armstrong, and the Erikson TEC Center for all the fantastic resources and professional development opportunities.

I'm indebted to the many robotics and computer science instructors at the Center for Talent Development (CTD) who have informed my work. Years ago, Eric Simon was the first robotics teacher I ever observed. I watched his fourth graders struggle to build and program a LEGO Mindstorms robot that would open a door. None of them were successful, but it was one of the most powerful and challenging learning experiences I had ever seen. From "How Things Work" instructor Tony Perry I learned the value of taking machines apart. I learned about Scratch programming from Brian Myers, Stephen Blood, and David Green. More recently, when we began piloting robotics and coding courses in the early childhood classrooms of the CTD summer Leapfrog program, I benefited from the feedback and ideas I received from teachers like Amanda Burns, Nina Diehl, Tess Heerema, Leah Johnston, Amy Lindgren, Victoria Livingston, and Kathleen Mercury. Thank you, also, to the Northwestern University faculty members on the Leapfrog Advisory Committee, in particular Dr. Michael Peshkin for robotics and mechanical engineering expertise, Dr. Michael Horn for his understanding of thoughtful uses of emerging technologies, Dr. David Uttal and Kinari Atit for insights on spatial cognition and symbolic representations, and Dr. Alexis Lauricella and Sarah Pila for expertise on the impact of media technology on young children. And, of course, I'm very grateful to the young children I taught and observed as I developed and piloted the activities in this book. They were my best teachers.

Thank you to my editors and friends at Redleaf Press, including David Heath, Laurie Herrmann, Kara Lomen, and Christine Zuchora-Walske. And finally, thank you to my family for their love and support. As I wrote this book, I often thought of my brother Mark and his passion for computers and engineering from a young age. I remember how, when we were kids in the 1970s, he used to carry a big box of punch cards to an after-school computer club. Can you believe how far we've come?

Introduction

Simone and the Evil Robot

As early childhood professionals, we can learn a lot about how children think by observing their play. Sometimes an observation will reveal what children understand about robots. Here's an example: Simone, age five, and Daniel, age four, are playing together on their preschool playground. The day is cold and windy, but the children are warm, bundled into heavy coats, snow pants, and boots.

"You be my puppy, Daniel," says Simone.

"Beep, beep!" replies Daniel, swinging his arms stiffly. "I'm not a puppy. I'm a robot."

Simone says, "You can be a robot puppy."

Daniel plops down onto the frozen grass and crawls on all fours. "Ruff, ruff! Beep, beep!" He shouts, "Ruff, beep, ruff, beep! I'm a robot puppy!"

Simone watches him and smiles. "Okay, puppy robot, come here! Come and sit."

Daniel crawls to Simone's feet. The heavy snow pants slow his movements. This makes his progress seem even more mechanical and robotlike.

"Ouch," says Daniel as his knees bump a stick.

"Hurry, puppy. Sit here," says Simone.

"Beep, beep, beep!" Daniel sits on his haunches and looks up at Simone.

"Roll over, puppy robot!" Simone commands.

Daniel looks at the cold ground covered with sticks and rocks. "No! Beep, beep, no roll over!"

"You have to do it," says Simone. "You're my robot puppy."

"No," repeats Daniel, shaking his head.

"Then I'll unplug your battery and turn off your wires," counters Simone.

"So what?" says Daniel. "I'm not that kind of a robot puppy. I'm an *evil* robot puppy." He stands up. "I can do whatever I want! I'm going to crash the whole world!" Daniel runs away, laughing. Simone scowls at him, but soon she takes off too, happily following Daniel. The chase is on, and a new game has begun.

This observation of Daniel and Simone demonstrates what these children understand and believe about robots. The children's pretend play and conversations show that they both have an interest in robots, as do many young children. Robots loom large in modern media—in movies, television shows, and digital games. Both children and adults often encounter robot characters in advertising and popular culture.

But what specific concepts do Daniel and Simone understand about robots? Let's look more closely at what they said and how they played. The interaction between Simone and Daniel the robot puppy demonstrates that both children understand the concept of commands. People control robots by commands. This means that when you tell the robot what to do, the robot will do what you say. At least it's supposed to! Daniel's robot puppy was not so obedient, but real working robots are programmed to comply with specific commands.

Simone's comment "Then I'll unplug your battery and turn off your wires" demonstrates another accurate understanding about robots. She knows that robots have a power source. In real life, as well as in pretend play, batteries often power robots.

The children's actions and comments in this scenario also demonstrate a common misunderstanding about robots: robots can defy commands. Daniel pretends that his robot is "evil," or dangerous. It's true that robots, or really any electronic devices, often frustrate us when they don't work properly. But robots are machines made by people and programmed to do what people tell them to do. They are not monsters. One of our challenges and responsibilities as educators is teaching children accurate information and dispelling misconceptions. Robotics activities like the ones in this book will help children develop scientifically accurate understandings of the advanced technology in the world around them.

The Daniel and Simone scenario also demonstrates how to effectively engage young children in science, technology, engineering, and math (STEM) learning: through play and through stories. The activities in this book will introduce children to computer science, coding, and robotics concepts using child-centered and play-based experiences that are grounded in developmentally appropriate practices.

Why Robotics?

If you look around you right now, do you see any robots? You may not be sitting next to an evil robot puppy like our young friend Daniel, but you probably are not far from a programmable electronic device, such as a laptop, tablet, or smartphone. You may also be near a programmable thermostat, an alarm clock, a coffeemaker, or other common household appliance. Robotic devices—in other words, machines programmed by computer code—are all around us. Robots vacuum floors and assemble cars. They frost cupcakes in factories and see through walls at construction sites. Robots can even help doctors perform surgery.

We teach children about the weather, about the rain that splashes onto their boots and the sun that warms their skin. We teach children about plants and animals, about the seeds that grow into tall trees and the pets that make them smile. We teach children about stories and counting, about letters and numbers, building a foundation of skills for later success in reading and math. But computer science topics, such as coding and robotics, are rarely included in an early childhood curriculum. Even in kindergarten through grade twelve, exposure to computer science is limited (Google Inc. and Gallup Inc. 2016). So why don't we teach young children about machines and computers, about the robots and devices that make their lives safer, easier, and perhaps more interesting and more entertaining? Prior to 2010, when the launch of the Apple iPad heralded a new wave of accessible devices with touch screens and other child-friendly features, we simply didn't have the tools to teach computer science using developmentally appropriate practices. Now we do, but most early childhood teachers do not yet have the training, experience, models, and resources to know how to teach tech topics to young children. This book is an effort to change that. Here you'll find basic explanations so you can understand introductory computer science concepts well enough to engage in conversations with young children. You'll also find guidelines and tips for using developmentally appropriate computer science activities in early childhood classrooms.

Let's start from square one. The field of robotics engineering involves two kinds of work: building robots and programming robots. Building robots requires knowledge of design engineering as well as mechanical and electrical engineering. Programming robots requires knowledge of coding and computer science. These terms and topics—"computer science," "coding," "robotics," "engineering"—can sound intimidating, even to adults. Early childhood educators, especially those who are baby boomers or members of Generation X, are not always confident in their own understanding of computer science terms. Many adults are digital immigrants, while the children we teach are often digital natives. A digital immigrant is someone who grew up without access to personal computers, tablets, and smartphones—someone (like me) who had to learn how to use these tools intentionally, as an adult. A digital native is someone who never knew a world without these tools. For example, have you ever noticed how some young children today will often walk up to an ordinary TV and swipe at the screen with their fingers, as if the TV screen were a touch screen? Children born after 2010, the year the iPad was introduced, often develop expectations and understandings of electronic devices that many of us digital immigrants never consider. And yet we still have a responsibility, as educators, to prepare children to be successful in the twenty-first-century world in which they live, even if this task challenges us to learn something new ourselves.

Rest assured that we can teach young children about robotics using the same developmentally appropriate methods and practices we use to teach children about other subjects. Keep in mind that we are building the foundation for later learning. It's a foundation of skills and experiences that children can use later, for more advanced studies of computer science and design engineering. We are not reinventing *how* we teach, only adding some new ideas regarding *what* we teach. We are building a foundation and creating a pathway for later learning.

Let's look at it this way. We don't teach preschoolers geometry, but we do teach them about triangles. We teach them that a triangle has three sides, that triangles come in different sizes. We teach young children that a triangle can have a corner, or angle, that's just like a corner of a square (a right angle). We teach them that triangles can be placed together to make other shapes, such as squares or even stars. We can agree that it is developmentally appropriate to teach children these concepts about triangles—through play, through games, through stories, and maybe even through some teacher-facilitated lessons or demonstrations. It would be silly to make children wait for a high school geometry class to learn about triangles. We know that triangles are all around them every day.

The same is true of robotics and computer science. Children see and sometimes even use machines and computers, smartphones and robots, all around them every day. It would be silly to make them wait until they take computer science classes in high school or college to learn the basic concepts. We can easily introduce them to foundational computer science concepts through play, through games, through stories, and maybe even through some teacher-facilitated lessons or demonstrations.

The Innovation Economy

Another important reason for introducing robotics to young children is the urgent need for innovative and independent thinkers in a technology- and information-driven economy. If the twentieth century was the age of industry, then the twenty-first century is the age of information. Young children today are growing up in a time when any question they can think up will have a thousand answers on the web. Our responsibility as educators is to help them make sense of all this information. We must teach them how to think critically about the sources of information, how to choose what information is important and true, and how to make good use of the information they have. As Alison Gopnik argues in her *New York Times* opinion piece "What Babies Know about Physics and Foreign Languages," the challenges children will face in the future will require a creative learning process that sparks curiosity and innovation rather than a traditional teacher-directed learning process. Gopnik writes, "Parents and policy makers care about teaching because they recognize that learning is increasingly important in an information age. But the new information economy, as opposed to the older industrial one, demands more innovation and less imitation, more creativity and less conformity" (Gopnik 2016). The activities in this book support this kind of learning. I can't think of a better example of innovative and creative learning than figuring out how to build and program a robot.

Computer Science as a Core Subject Area

Don't just take my word for it. Leaders and researchers at all levels of the US education system recognize that STEM learning must be a top priority in order to prepare students for twenty-first-century careers. The National Math and Science Initiative (NMSI) reports that in 2018, the United States will be short as many as three million high-skilled workers in STEM fields (NMSI, accessed 2017). Robotics is a topic that incorporates all aspects of STEM learning: science (physics), technology (coding), engineering (design, mechanical, and electrical), and math (geometry, data, algorithms). The study of robotics aligns well with Common Core State Standards (CCSS) and Next Generation Science Standards (NGSS) that emphasize critical thinking, communication, collaboration, and creativity. In particular, the coding aspects of robotics help prepare children for higher-level computer science studies, a top priority for many school districts such as Chicago Public Schools, where computer science is now a required core subject area (CPS 2016).

Computer Science Framework

Fortunately, we now have an important new tool for creating computer science curricula and developing plans and policies for computer science learning. This tool, the *K–12 Computer Science Framework*, was developed through a collaboration of key technology education organizations, such as the Computer Science Teachers Association, NMSI, and Code.org. The *Framework*, released in October 2016, provides conceptual guidelines to inform the development of computer science standards and curriculum and build capacity for teaching computer science (K12CSF 2016).

While the *Framework* focuses on grades kindergarten through twelve, it includes a detailed chapter on computer science in early childhood education. This chapter is readable and affirming to early childhood teachers who are familiar with developmentally appropriate practice. For example, one of the essential statements of the *Framework* is the assertion that play is the pedagogical bedrock of all early learning environments (K12CSF 2016). In fact, the *Framework* presents play as one of five "powerful ideas" that are relevant and significant in computer science learning at the early childhood level. These five ideas are play, patterns, problem solving, representation, and sequencing. The framework authors state that when these five powerful ideas are applied to computer science, learning becomes "a natural extension of children's everyday engagement with their environment and builds on what educators already do in their daily practice" (K12CSF 2016, 185).

Powerful Ideas

The term "powerful ideas" in the context of computer science learning is not a new one. Seymour Papert, author of the groundbreaking book *Mindstorms: Children, Computers, and Powerful Ideas*, coined this term (Papert 1980). More recently, "powerful ideas" has been a core concept in the work of Marina Umaschi Bers, a pioneer of early childhood robotics. Bers elaborates on the meaning and use of the term "powerful ideas" in the context of children's early learning experiences in robotics. She states that powerful ideas "afford new ways of thinking" related to both content and process—both *what* children learn and *how* they learn it (Bers 2008, 23). For example, activity 1.7 in this book involves taking apart a clock. The powerful ideas children may develop during this activity are related both to what parts the children discover inside the clock (gears, a spring, a bell, a pendulum) and to the learning process itself (deconstruction—the taking apart of things to reveal new information and new questions).

The emphasis on play as a powerful idea in pre-K computer science aligns the *Framework* with developmentally appropriate practices in obvious ways. An examination of the other powerful ideas demonstrates additional connections with the core concepts of high-quality early childhood education: patterns, problem solving, representation, and sequencing. Recognizing and creating patterns helps children make sense of their world when they organize objects and information using common features (Bers 2008). Children engage in problem-solving processes every day; these experiences become valuable learning opportunities when they make mistakes and construct new knowledge through trial and error, and when their teachers help facilitate learning and reflection through open-ended questions (Bers 2008). Children learn representation when they use symbols, such as letters of the alphabet, to represent sounds and meaning. Similarly, in computer science, many different kinds of symbols (such as arrows, shapes, text, and numbers) can represent algorithms (Bers 2008). The final powerful idea, sequencing, is already a core concept in any early childhood curriculum. When children learn to get dressed or sing a song or tell a story, they are learning a sequence. In computer science as well, children learn to arrange events, ideas, and objects in a specific order to achieve a desired outcome.

Computational Thinking

Beyond the pre-K level, the *Framework* emphasizes the importance of developing computational thinking. Computational thinking refers to strategic ways of thinking, such as breaking a large problem into smaller pieces for analysis. Computational thinking does not mean thinking like a computer. Rather, it means thinking in ways that allow you to use a computer effectively as a tool.

Here's an example of computational thinking at the preschool level. Suppose a group of children are playing in the block corner, constructing a garage for toy cars. One of the children suggests they build a ramp so the cars can drive from the floor up to the roof. These particular children have built ramps before, and they know that in addition to the usual rectangle blocks (units) and square blocks (half units), they will need a lot of triangle or wedge blocks to build a ramp. All the blocks are in sloppy piles around the floor, and one of the children decides to take on the job of triangle hunter. She crawls around on the floor collecting half a dozen triangle blocks in a basket. Armed with an ample supply of triangle blocks, she begins the ramp construction. With very little conversation—simply a shared understanding of how to build a ramp—this group of children used computational thinking to evaluate the task ahead of them. The child who collected the triangle blocks identified one of the key challenges (finding enough triangles), and by collecting the essential pieces in one place, she enabled the group to complete the task more efficiently.

Breaking down a task into key pieces is the kind of analysis that's an important element in computational thinking. Children need to experience this type of problem solving to develop a foundation of skills and understandings that prepare them for more advanced computer science and robotics learning later in their schooling. As this example illustrates, computational thinking is a way of analyzing a problem. While people can learn computational thinking without a computer, an ability to apply computational thinking to complex tasks and problems is useful in learning computer programming.

Constructivism and Developmentally Appropriate Practice

While we can all probably agree that computer science is an important area of study in the twenty-first century, many educators and families still feel some discomfort about including robotics in an early childhood curriculum. I recall my own experience years ago, when I was working as the director of a child care program that was affiliated with a Mennonite congregation. The culture and traditions of this program—demonstrated in each classroom by the simple wooden toys, the plants indoors, the garden outdoors, and the prevalence of natural materials and fabrics in the environment—did not allow for any consideration of computers in the classroom. Of course, this was in the 1990s, when classroom computers were huge and children had to manipulate a keyboard or mouse to play a simple game. The electronic devices available for young children now, as you will see in chapter 3, are much more accessible and more appropriate for children's bodies and minds.

While it may seem like these devices have appeared quite suddenly, the progress toward developmentally appropriate technology has been a slow, steady journey, traveled by many great minds. In fact, we can easily trace the robotic devices on the cutting edge today, such as the Bee-Bot or Cubetto robots described in chapter 3, back to Jean Piaget and the core of a constructivist education philosophy. David Elkind, renowned child psychologist, details this path in the foreword to Bers's book *Blocks to Robots: Learning with Technology in the Early Childhood Classroom*. Elkind describes Piaget, the creator of constructivism, a theory of cognitive development centering on the idea that children learn through direct physical experience, through play and through their interactions with their environment. Piaget mentored Papert, and Papert mentored Bers (Bers 2008). Both Papert and Bers, as I mentioned earlier, have used the term "powerful ideas" to describe the wide impact of computer science experiences on other kinds of learning. The Piaget-Papert-Bers pathway is a direct link from the original development of constructivist theory to the hands-on robotics activities and curricula springing up today everywhere you look.

Bers and her colleagues, such as Michael Horn at the DevTech Lab at Tufts University, use the term "tangible programming" or "tangible tech" to describe the hands-on constructivist experiences now available to young children. Bers and Horn write, "Our work is rooted in notions of developmentally appropriate practice (DAP), a perspective within early childhood education concerned with creating learning environments sensitive to children's social, emotional, physical, and cognitive development" (Bers and Horn 2010, 50). My own experience developing and implementing robotics curricula with young children supports this notion. When given the right tools, young children can engage in developmentally appropriate computer science and engineering activities.

If developmentally appropriate robots seem surprising or implausible to you, you're not alone. In 2009, after twenty years of teaching and directing preschool and child care programs, I took a position as a program coordinator at Northwestern University's Center for Talent Development (CTD). My job was, and still is, to develop and implement enrichment courses for academically gifted and talented children. I run programs for children as young as three years old. Previously, my areas of expertise in curriculum were language and literacy. In my position at CTD, my work has focused on STEM topics. I came to the right place at the right time. I began developing computer science and robotics curricula for young children just as developmentally appropriate devices and apps became available for classroom use. When I started working at CTD, our coding and robotics courses were pretty much limited to Lego robotics and Scratch animation at the third- and fourth-grade levels. But by 2015 we began offering coding and robotics courses at all levels, starting at pre-K. We were able to do this because developmentally appropriate tools like Bee-Bots and apps like Kodable became more readily available. I've now developed and implemented coding and robotics courses at the pre-K level in many different settings, which have reached hundreds of children. The activities in this book are a result of that experience.

Preparing to Teach Robotics

You don't need to know about robotics or computer science to begin implementing the activities in this book. Any teacher with an open mind, a curiosity about how things work, and the ability to ask good questions can generate the powerful ideas described by Bers. Teaching robotics to young children requires a disposition, not a credential. By "disposition," I mean a state of readiness, a readiness to engage with children in a problem-solving process. This disposition is so much more important than content knowledge. That's because the specific content of robotics and computer science curricula—the devices, the hardware, the apps, and the programming languages—is constantly evolving and changing. People are continually developing new technologies. The robotics landscape will already be different and new by the time you finish reading this book. The best way to prepare ourselves to teach in this changing landscape is to nurture and demonstrate an openness to learning and a willingness to engage in problem-solving processes.

Another important disposition is a willingness to learn from children. We must abandon the notion that we, as teachers, are always the experts. Remember, many of us are digital immigrants teaching digital natives. Although robotics and coding are topics I've studied for years, when I'm teaching technology to young children, I often find myself in a position where the children know more than I do. For many early childhood teachers, that position can be very uncomfortable. We are accustomed to being the fountains of knowledge in our classrooms. "This is how you tie your shoes. This fruit is called an apricot. Birds fly south in the winter." But young children today have an advantage over us when it comes to technology. They are often brave when we are cautious. They fearlessly experiment with and master new technological devices and tasks. That fearlessness—the ability to experiment rapidly with trial and error—often allows children to learn new technology concepts more quickly than adults can.

Letting go of being the expert is hard. For guidance in this, we can look to our colleagues in gifted education. Teachers who work with academically gifted and talented children are more accustomed than early childhood educators to the experience of teaching students who are smarter than the teachers themselves are. For example, imagine teaching a classroom of students who can read fluently at age four, perform calculus at age seven, or breeze through a whole year of high school chemistry in three weeks at age twelve. Working in gifted education requires teachers who are able to serve as guides and facilitators, not experts.

Through my experience in both early childhood education and gifted education, I've come up with a way to describe teaching from a disposition that's open to learning alongside children, as their guide and facilitator. I like to call it "relationship-based robotics." As we introduce children to the topics of robotic engineering and computer science, we are in a collaborative relationship with the children, learning along with them. Our role as teachers is to guide the process of discovery, provide meaningful and accurate resources, ask great questions, and be prepared to respond and to listen.

The word "relationship" in the term "relationship-based robotics" refers to the relationships in the classroom—between you and the children, among the children themselves, and between the children and the other mentors and helpers they encounter through the learning process, such as parents and neighborhood experts. The word "relationship" also refers to the relationships among the experiences and concepts of robotics activities. While each activity has its individual value, the role of the teacher in a relationship-based robotics curriculum is to help children make connections among diverse experiences.

In addition, the word "relationship" refers to the relationships between the robotics learning in the early childhood classroom and the larger robotics and computer science issues and concepts in the world outside the classroom. In relationship-based robotics, we are teaching children to be good digital citizens. We can do this by helping them think about what kind of world we are creating with tech tools. We hope that what children learn about computer science when they are young will ultimately help them understand and improve the world in which we live. The young children in our classrooms today may someday figure out how technological tools can help keep people healthy, protect the environment, or make other important changes and improvements. As early childhood educators, our role is to empower children to be innovators and creators, not passive consumers of whatever new tech gadgets come along. Ethical questions about how to change the world for the better are at the heart of relationship-based robotics. The activities in chapter 4 address these questions directly. Even very young children can think about how robots might help make people safer and healthier. Even preschoolers can use critical thinking to evaluate whether a robot, toy, or app is useful, helpful, or beautiful.

Give Me Back My Caps!

When I began learning more about technology and how to teach young children computer science concepts, I was surprised to discover that I actually knew more than I thought I did. You too may find that you already know a lot about computer science, coding, and robotics. In my work training teachers to implement technology programs, I've found that teachers, especially old-school teachers like me, feel reassured when we can connect familiar classroom tools and activities with innovations in robotics and computer science. I like to use the picture book *Caps for Sale* to demonstrate these connections.

Caps for Sale, written by Esphyr Slobodkina and first published in 1940, is the story of a peddler who sells caps. Many early childhood teachers have fond associations with this book. They may remember it from their own childhoods or from reading it to children in class. When I am conducting a teacher workshop on the topic of technology and I pull out a worn copy of *Caps for Sale*, the teachers visibly relax. Here is something they know, something that feels familiar and comfortable.

Before we review the story together, I ask the teachers, "How is the experience of the peddler similar to the experience of a computer programmer?" I ask them to take a moment to imagine a computer programmer at work. What does the programmer do all day? Often the teachers imagine someone sitting in a cubicle, looking at a screen, tapping lines of code on a keyboard. How could this image have anything in common with Slobodkina's old peddler in *Caps for Sale*?

In the story, the peddler carries his wares, the caps, on the top of his head, stacked one on top of the other. The peddler always stacks the caps in the same order: first his own checked cap, then the gray caps, then the brown caps, then the blue caps, and then the red caps on top. One day the peddler encounters a frustrating challenge. He takes a nap under a tree and wakes to discover that while he was sleeping, a group of monkeys stole his caps. The tree was filled with monkeys, and each monkey wore one of the peddler's caps.

The peddler shakes his finger at the monkeys and commands them, "You monkeys you, you give me back my caps!" (Slobodkina 1987, 30). The monkeys, of course, shake their fingers back at him, mirroring his actions. Then the peddler begins to get frustrated, and the situation escalates. He shakes his fists and shouts, and he stamps his feet. In each case, the monkeys imitate his actions. They do not give the peddler his caps. At last the peddler becomes so angry that he takes his own checked cap off his head, throws it on the ground, and begins to walk away. Then what do the monkeys do? They take off their caps and throw them to the ground! The peddler is able to collect his caps and return to his rounds.

How is the experience of the peddler similar to the experience of a computer programmer? Most of us can recognize that the peddler uses a series of commands to try to get what he wants. The word "command" is a programming term, but even those of us who don't work with computers have heard the word before. Also familiar is the level of frustration the peddler experiences. Many of us have become angry while trying in vain to accomplish something with a computer. The peddler's experience with the monkeys is remarkably similar to the debugging or troubleshooting process a programmer might use to try to solve a problem with computer code.

Who would have guessed that a popular picture book published more than seventy-five years ago would demonstrate core computer science concepts such as commands and troubleshooting? And yet, it does. As you can see, many of the ideas at the core of computer science and robotics learning may already be familiar to early childhood educators. But perhaps we simply haven't encountered them in a technological context. Remember, a key disposition for teaching robotics to young children is a willingness to abandon the role of the expert. We are all learning together. Our job is to guide the children along the path, but we will all walk the path together.

Basic Terms and Concepts

Robotics activities fall under the category of STEM learning. Every robotics activity has some connection to each of the four STEM subject areas, but technology and engineering are probably the most obvious connections. The term "technology" is often used synonymously with the term "computer science." The formal definition of "technology" includes any kind of machine or equipment invented to solve a problem (such as a wind-up alarm clock), while the formal definition of "computer science" is restricted to the study of devices that are programmed by computer code. Informally, however, people often use both terms to refer to anything related to computers and electronics. In this book, I'll usually use the term "technology" broadly to include both computer science and engineering, such as mechanical engineering, and "computer science" to refer specifically to computer programming–related topics. The term "coding" is often used broadly to mean all things related to computers, but coding is actually a more specific task. To code, or to write code, means to program a computer. You may be familiar with the term "code" as related to secret codes or Morse code. A code is a sequence of symbols, such as letters or numbers, that represent meaning. Coding in computer science is an active process in which the programmer makes decisions about what to accomplish and then writes or creates a code to make that happen. Some of the robotics devices introduced in chapter 3 involve coding at an introductory level.

What makes robotics so exciting for young children is that a robot is a tangible thing that can be built or moved or manipulated in some way. The three-dimensional, real-world characteristics and processes of robotics involve engineering—the "E" in "STEM." Building robots and robotic devices may involve many different subcategories of engineering, depending on the materials and structures used. These different kinds of engineering include mechanical engineering, electrical engineering, and design engineering. For most young children, these tangible, concrete aspects of building, manipulating, and maneuvering are more meaningful than the abstract coding aspects. For this reason, we'll focus on engineering first, in chapter 2, before we move on to coding or programming activities in chapter 3.

How to Use This Book

The activities in this book are presented in five chapters. The activities appear in an intentional sequence. This sequence builds a foundation of understanding introductory robotics concepts to prepare children for a lifetime of learning in computer science and engineering. In general, the sequence progresses from the familiar to the novel, from what children already know about their world to ideas and experiences that may be new. And yet there's no need to follow the exact order of activities in this book. Use the table of contents to choose the activities that seem most relevant to the interests and abilities of the children in your care. Dip in and out, experiment, and see what works for you. Model an open and investigative process for the children as you explore the concepts and materials in this book.

Think of this book as a cookbook. Skip around and try the activities that seem most intriguing and appealing to you and the children. The activities in chapter 1 ("What Is a Robot?") are like appetizers, whetting the children's interest in robots. Chapter 2 ("How Do We Build Robots?") is like the first course, a beginning yet satisfying portion of robotics information and experiences. Chapter 3 ("How Do We Tell Robots What to Do?") is like the main course. The activities in this chapter, which introduce real coding experiences with actual robotic devices, are the real meat of the book. Chapter 4 ("How Do Robots Help Us?") is like the dessert, adding an extra layer of understanding of how robots can make the world a sweeter and better place. Finally, chapter 5 ("How Can We Learn More about Robots?") is like a late-night snack—some added taste and nutrition that comes later, after the meal has been digested.

Here is a brief description of the core content of each chapter:

Chapter 1: What Is a Robot?

The activities in this chapter foster creative and critical thinking about what makes a robot a robot. We can emphasize some core characteristics (robots are programmed by people, robots have power, robots have jobs to do) when we introduce children to robotics, but children's own original ideas, observations, and definitions are valuable and important too.

Chapter 2: How Do We Build Robots?

The activities in this chapter focus on engineering. Most involve hands-on, open-ended construction with a variety of materials. These experiences introduce children to core ideas in physics and engineering, such as simple machines and the design engineering process.

Chapter 3: How Do We Tell Robots What to Do?

People tell robots what to do through programming, also known as coding. We give robots commands using different kinds of programming languages. The activities in this chapter introduce children to coding-related concepts, such as identifying patterns and creating a sequence. You can conduct many of these activities without specialized equipment. This chapter also provides guidance for introducing children to tangible tech devices like Bee-Bots and Cubetto, as well as introductory coding apps such as Kodable and ScratchJr.

Chapter 4: How Do Robots Help Us?

At the core of relationship-based robotics is the idea that we can use robots to help change the world and make it better. The activities in this chapter focus on how robots can help people, animals, and our environment. These activities are intended for children who have already had some experience thinking about robots and who enjoy imagining what they can do with robots.

Chapter 5: How Can We Learn More about Robots?

The activities and resources in this chapter provide guidance on helping children transition from an introductory understanding of computer science to higher-level learning in elementary, middle, and high school. These ideas could also be meaningful for children in after-school enrichment programs.

The Hundred Languages of Children

The activities in this book can function within many different curriculum models. They lend themselves easily to theme-based curriculum units on the topics of robots, machines, building, construction, and so on. For teachers working in programs that use an emergent curriculum model or a project-based model, these activities can serve as your go-to resource when children demonstrate an interest in how things work. In my own experience learning about and practicing project-based learning experiences, I am frequently inspired by the Reggio Emilia concept of the "hundred languages of children." Loris Malaguzzi, the visionary founder of Italy's Reggio Emilia schools, famously said that children have a hundred different ways of thinking, playing, speaking, and listening. Robotics activities inspire children to develop even more new languages—languages made up of codes and patterns, of metal and blocks, of shapes and movements. The concept of the hundred languages aligns perfectly with the powerful idea of representation in the *Framework*.

While some early childhood teachers may fear that introducing technology to young children will silence their creativity, the Reggio Emilia schools have proven otherwise. In the book *The Hundred Languages of Children: The Reggio Emilia Experience in Transformation*, there is a wonderful story describing the meaningful and developmentally appropriate use of robotics in an emergent project. The children observed from a classroom window that during a storm, a branch had broken from a tree. The children wanted to find a way for the branch to communicate with its "mother," the tree. With guidance from their teachers, the children were able to use a robotics kit to record an audio track and attach a light sensor to the branch so that when the sun rose each morning, the branch would say to the tree, "Good morning, Mommy" (Forman 2012, 345). This is the kind of meaningful experience at the heart of relationship-based robotics.

1

What Is a Robot?

The Important Thing about Robots

The Important Book, written by Margaret Wise Brown and illustrated by Leonard Weisgard, was first published in 1949. The book describes the essential heart of everyday objects or experiences with poetic simplicity. "The important thing about a spoon is that you eat with it. It's like a little shovel. . . . The important thing about rain is that it is wet" (Brown 1999, 1–4). If Margaret Wise Brown were writing *The Important Book* today, I think she might include something like this: "The important thing about a robot is that you program it. It's a machine that will do what you tell it to do. A robot might have a face or arms, but it's not alive. You use a computer to tell the robot what to do. But the important thing about a robot is that you program it."

The activities in this chapter help teachers observe and listen to children to gain some understanding of what children already know and believe about robots. These activities also promote children's critical thinking about what makes a robot a robot and dispel some of the misconceptions about robots. One misconception both children and adults often hold is that robots might, at any moment, become crazed or evil, out of control, on the fritz. The image of the evil or dangerously malfunctioning robot has been a staple of stories in popular culture for a long time, especially since the creepy robotic computer HAL in Stanley Kubrick's 1968 film *2001: A Space Odyssey*. The image of the evil robot appears in children's literature and media as well, from the out-of-control robot in Katie Van Camp's picture book *CookieBot!* to the evil robots in the animated Transformers movies. Children and adults need to know that robots are machines invented and programmed by humans. We tell robots what to do by creating commands in the form of computer code. Most of the activities in this chapter are open-ended and give children opportunities to develop their own imaginative ideas and inventions. But one core idea teachers can emphasize is this notion that people build and control robots, and that every child has the power to learn how to become a robotics engineer.

Activity 1.1
Famous Robots

Many young children already have some ideas about what a robot is and what a robot can do. They've seen TV shows and movies about robots, such as BB-8 from *Star Wars: The Force Awakens*. Most, if not all, of these robot characters are fictional, but they may have some features and characteristics that are based on existing technology. Asking questions about these famous robot characters will help reveal children's thinking about robots. These conversations may also help children discover and identify the important and essential characteristics of robots. Conversations about famous robots on TV or in movies will also challenge children to develop critical thinking skills about what's real and possible and what's pretend and unlikely to happen in real life. These conversations can be both reassuring and inspiring for children.

As you discuss famous robots, you can build your conversations around these big questions:

▸ What kinds of robots are in books, on TV, in movies, or in video games?

▸ Are robots real?

▸ How can we figure out what's real and what's pretend?

▸ What is a robot, anyway?

These conversations may come up spontaneously, when children talk about a movie they saw or when a child comes to school with a robot T-shirt or toy. You can use this opportunity as a teachable moment and begin a conversation about robots on the spot. These conversations can take place in groups or one-on-one. A smaller rather than larger group of children at a center or during snack would probably work best for developing conversations in which everyone can participate.

A conversation about famous robots could also be a preplanned activity at story time or in a learning center. Find a picture book, movie poster, or action figure that represents a robot from a well-known movie or story. The Star Wars robots are well known among young children. Some other robot characters they might know include Baymax from the movie *Big Hero 6*, WALL-E or EVE from the movie *WALL-E*, Rodney Copperbottom from the movie *Robots*, Rescue Bots from the Transformers cartoons, the robot dog Goddard in *The Adventures of Jimmy Neutron* TV show, Rolie Polie Olie from the William Joyce picture book and TV show *Rolie Polie Olie*, or the robot dog from the PBS Kids show *Ready Jet Go!*

This activity is simply about having meaningful conversations with children. Conversations about robots can be long or short. You may begin a conversation about robots one day, without much interest from the children. And then another day, you find that something sparks the children's imagination, and you're able to have a much longer conversation.

These conversations are informal preassessments of children's thinking. Asking children open-ended questions about robots will tell you what they already know about robots and what they want to know. Listening carefully to their answers will provide helpful guidance and insights as you prepare to teach the other activities in this book.

You may want to document these conversations by taking notes, writing down children's responses word for word, or recording the conversations with audio or video recordings or digital photographs.

Here are some discussion questions about robots you can ask children:

▷ (Point to a robot picture or toy.) Have you seen this robot before? What can you tell me about this robot?

▷ What can this robot do?

▷ Can this robot talk and make noises? What does this robot say?

▷ Can this robot move around? How does it move?

▷ Where does this robot live?

▷ What is this robot made of?

▷ Is this robot real or pretend? How do you know?

- ► How is this robot similar to a real, living person? How is it different from a person?

- ► Do you like this robot? Why or why not?

Be aware that some children may have had experiences viewing robot movies or shows that are frightening for young children, such as the Terminator movies. If children express or show fear and anxiety about these robots, the role of the teacher is to be direct and reassuring, emphasizing that these robots are not real and can't hurt them. Teachers can share with families the fears children express in these conversations, along with positive feedback about the importance of listening to children and establishing what they already know and understand about robots.

If children show an interest in expanding the conversations, create a robot photo album or poster. Print out images of robots and invite children to arrange and glue them onto paper. Ask children to dictate labels and descriptions of each robot. Put the pages together into a book or display them as posters.

Activity 1.2
Machine Faces

While most of the robots children see in the media are humanoid, many real robots do not have faces. Young children may have a hard time understanding that a robot doesn't have to have a face. This activity, which promotes critical thinking, will help children develop an understanding that there is more than one way for a robot to look. This understanding will build a foundation for deeper explorations of robotics later on.

This activity also plays with the ways in which people tend to personify machines and inanimate objects. Humans seem to have a natural desire to see the human form and faces all around them. "Pareidolia" is the term for the human tendency to see faces or other familiar patterns in the environment. When you look at the pattern of bolts on your lawn mower and see them as two eyes, a nose, and a mouth, that's an example of pareidolia. In this activity, children can have some fun with the idea of machines with faces as you continue to explore the characteristics of robots.

As you explore the personification of machines with children, here are some big questions to consider and discuss:

- ▷ Do robots always have faces?

- ▷ Can a machine have a face?

- ▷ What is a face? Why do people need faces?

This activity may arise as a spontaneous teachable moment, when a conversation leads to the topic of faces. This could also be a planned activity or a discussion for circle time or a learning center. To prepare, collect images of machines with faces. Here are some sources you could use:

- ● www.technocrazed.com/amazing-faces-hidden-in-everyday-objects
  -photo-gallery

- ● www.dailymail.co.uk/news/article-2265793/Who-looking-Even
  -mundane-everyday-objects-reveal-friendly-face.html

- ● www.nydailynews.com/life-style/hidden-faces-everyday-objects
  -gallery-1.1248057

Visit these sites and prepare the photos in advance. Many websites have advertisements that are not appropriate for young children to view.

When you begin talking with children about robots, they may express the idea (based on what they've seen in movies or on TV) that robots share many physical characteristics with people. Many of the robot characters they've seen have arms, legs, and faces. This activity provides an opportunity to explore the idea that some robots and machines have faces or can be imagined with faces. It also provides an opportunity for children to compare robots to the machines they see in their own environment at school or at home.

Invite a small group of children to look at images of robot characters, perhaps revisiting the images from the previous activity. Ask children to identify the eyes, nose, and mouth on each robot face. Then show children a few images of hidden faces on machines and everyday objects, like those on the websites listed above.

Go on a face hunt around your classroom or school to see if children can find faces hidden in everyday objects. Take photos of what the children find. Use the results of your face hunt to encourage children to compare robots to familiar machines, such as clocks, cars, refrigerators, TVs, vacuum cleaners, and so on. Draw children's attention to how many machines they and their families use each day. Begin a list called "Machines We Know" and post it in the classroom. This list may be important later, when children are learning more about how things work.

Activity 1.3
Make a Robot Face

In the previous activity, children imagined faces on machines and appliances. In this activity, children add paper features to machines to create faces of their own design. Both of these activities build on children's natural tendency to personify objects. The activities provide opportunities to talk about the similarities and differences among people, machines, computers, and robots.

As you continue to explore the idea of robot faces with children, here are some questions to consider and discuss:

▶ Can a machine have a face?

▶ What is a face?

▶ What are the features on a face, and what do they do?

▶ Are machines like people? In what ways?

This activity, making robot faces, is a natural extension of the previous activity. In fact, the children may, at some point, spontaneously ask to add paper faces or features to machines once they start noticing the machines in their environment. To prepare for this activity, gather markers and sticky notes (or paper and tape) for making eyes, noses, and mouths to attach onto machines. (Avoid stickers or tape that would be difficult to remove later.)

To begin, invite the children to look for machines, computers, and appliances in their environment—both large and small, such as refrigerators, telephones, laptops, air conditioners, or clocks. Ask the children, "Does this machine have a face?" See if the machine already has any features that look like they could be eyes, a nose,

or a mouth. Have the children stick paper eyes, nose, or mouth to the machine to make it look like it has a face.

The children may also enjoy giving each machine a name and creating stories about the machines with faces. Ask questions that will inspire the children to think about the personalities of the machines. For example, ask, "If this machine could talk, what would it say?" Invite the children to dictate stories individually or as a group.

Don't be afraid to encourage children's imaginative and fictional ideas about machines, computers, and robots. This kind of activity builds a foundation for later robotics learning because it draws children's attention to the visible features of machines and the machine's parts and functions. If children ask questions or seem curious about how the machine works and how it is made, make note of these questions and begin an inquiry process for investigating the answers. Many of the activities in chapter 2 of this book ("How Do We Build Robots?") will use an inquiry-based learning process to help build children's knowledge of how machines and robots are made.

Activity 1.4
Talk Like a Robot

In the previous two activities, as the children imagine and create faces for the appliances and tech devices in their world, they are essentially making friends with machines. A natural extension of these experiences is to imagine what a machine would sound like if it could speak to us.

As you continue to explore the characteristics of machines and robots with children, here are some big questions to consider and ask:

▶ If a machine could talk, what would it say?

▶ What would a machine's voice sound like?

▶ Is a talking machine a robot?

▶ What language do robots use?

▶ What makes a robot a robot?

This activity is another natural extension of the previous activities, in which children imagine machines that have some of the same characteristics as people. The children may, at some point, spontaneously begin speaking in mechanical voices during these activities and conversations. They may have seen movies or animations in which machines or robots speak, and the children may have some preconceived notions about the tone, speed, and articulations of a robot voice or a machine voice.

For this activity there are no special materials to prepare ahead of time, but you may choose to make audio or video recordings of the children's voices and conversations.

To begin, point to a machine (with or without a face) in your school environment and ask the children, "If this machine could talk, what would it sound like?" Or point to one of the robot images or toys used in a previous activity and ask, "How does this robot talk?" Invite the children to talk like robots and machines. Children will likely speak in mechanical voices, with a flat tone and a slow, even pace. Describe what you hear. For example, "That voice sounds different from your regular voice. Your machine voice sounds very plain and flat. I don't hear any excitement in your voice when you talk like that." Ask the children, "How do you know a machine would talk like this?" and "Why would a robot have a voice like that?"

The purpose of this activity is to generate interest in the characteristics, functions, and structures of machines and robots. You don't need to explain to the children exactly how robot voices are generated, though some children will have ideas about that. Make note of children's observations, guesses, and ideas as you continue to nurture their curiosity about robots and how they work.

The children may enjoy trying out their robot voices during regular classroom activities. Invite the children to sing a familiar song, such as "Twinkle, Twinkle, Little Star," in their robot voices. The children may also enjoy pretending to move like robots. Choose a song with motions, such as "Head and Shoulders, Knees and Toes," and invite the children to move like robots. Or, the next time your group is making a transition, such as going outdoors to play, invite the children to walk like robots. Later, when children learn more about how real robots move, you can look back on these earlier understandings and make comparisons and observations about what the children are learning about robots.

Activity 1.5
Robot Dance Party

Here's an active and kinesthetic way to extend children's thinking about robots and how they move: a robot dance party!

You can offer this activity as an option for free play, indoors or outdoors. The robot dance party also makes for a fun, active movement option on a cold or rainy day. You'll need a music source, such as a CD or digital music player, and plenty of room to dance. When you're selecting music for the robot dance party, you could choose any songs (from any genre) that are appropriate for young children. Electronic music, created using computers or synthesizers, is also a great choice. Children may be able to make a connection between the artificial sounds of electronic music and the artificial movements of a robot, especially if they have seen robots and heard electronic music as soundtracks on TV and in movies. A few examples of electronic instrumental music are the songs "Breaking Away" by the band Ratatat and "A New Error" by Moderat.

To begin, turn on the music and invite the children to dance "like robots." Some children may not have any prior knowledge or experience about how robots move, but some may have seen videos or cartoons of robots and may have some ideas about how a robot might move. If children need suggestions or ideas, here are some questions to ask:

- How do robots move?

- How is a robot different from a person? How is it the same?

- How would you dance if your legs were made out of metal or plastic?

- How would you dance if you had wheels instead of legs?

If you feel that the children need a visual prompt to help them think about how robots might move, show them a video of a Nao robot dancing. The Nao is a humanoid robot that has performed internationally with professional dancers. There are many Nao dance videos available online, such as this one: www.ted.com/talks/bruno_maisonnier_dance_tiny_robots.

Moving like robots leads naturally to deeper conversations about the characteristics of robots. Build conversations around open-ended questions. For example, ask, "What makes a robot move like that?" and "How are a robot's legs different from your legs?"

Make note of children's observations, guesses, or knowledge about the design and the materials of a robot, especially if children use specific terms for parts, such as "hinges" or "bolts" or "metal." You can explore and develop these terms and ideas in later activities.

Activity 1.6
Robot Picture Books

Finding a good read-aloud story about robots is a surprisingly difficult task. Most nonfiction books about robots are much too advanced for young children, and most fictional picture books don't demonstrate computer science or engineering concepts accurately. Few picture books offer engaging read-aloud stories that will spark creative, critical thinking around this essential question: "What is a robot?"

One notable exception is *Me and My Robot*, written by Tracey West and illustrated by Cindy Revell. This book tells the story of a boy named Reese as he and his robot work to help locate a lost kitten. Reese's robot begins the search by asking questions to find out the characteristics of a kitten. Although the text does not incorporate any programming terms, the lines of dialogue between Reese and his robot serve as the computer code or commands that direct the actions of the robot. After Reese explains to his robot that a kitten is an animal, the robot finds an animal—in this case, a big dog. The robot responded to the command to find an animal successfully, but now Reese must refine his code. Reese describes the kitten as small. Later, when even greater detail is needed to narrow the search, he tells the robot that a kitten is also soft and furry. Reese gives verbal commands to his robot in a manner that's similar to the way computer programmers write lines of code.

Here's a list of recommended robot picture books:

- *Boy and Bot* by Ame Dyckman
- *Clink* by Kelly DiPucchio
- *If I Had a Robot* by Dan Yaccarino
- *If I Had a Robot Dog* by Andrea Baruffi
- *I Like Robots* by Olga Kilicci
- *Mama Robot* by Davide Cali
- *Me and My Robot* by Tracey West
- *My Robot* by Eve Bunting
- *Rafa Was My Robot* by Alexandra Dellevoet
- *Robot Dog* by Mark Oliver
- *Robot Rumpus* by Sean Taylor
- *The Robot Alphabet* by Amanda Baehr Fuller
- *The Robot Book* by Heather Brown
- *Robots at Home* by Christine Zuchora-Walske
- *Robots Everywhere* by Denny Hebson
- *Robots, Robots Everywhere!* by Sue Fliess
- *Robot Zot!* by Jon Scieszka
- *Rolie Polie Olie* by William Joyce
- *Snowbots* by Aaron Reynolds
- *Wendel's Workshop* by Chris Riddell
- *Wodney Wat's Wobot* by Helen Lester

Before and after reading a robot picture book, ask the children questions such as these:

- What is a robot?

- How is a robot like a person?

- What can robots do?

- What materials do you think this robot is made of?

- How is this robot like a person? How is it like a machine?

Generate conversations that will help children make connections between the previous activities and the robots presented in the books. Note children's comments and questions about robots as documentation of the children's learning and thinking. Look for opportunities to develop a working definition of the word "robot." Begin a chart or poster with the phrase "A robot is" and create a running list of children's ideas. You can refer back to this list, add to it, and edit it as children's understanding of robots deepens and grows.

Activity 1.7
Take Apart a Machine or Robot

In this activity, you will demonstrate for the children how a simple machine can be taken apart. Any kind of take-apart activity provides an opportunity for children to learn how things work and to develop an understanding that machines and robots are made up of many different parts. Old clocks and fans make great take-aparts because they usually have large, visible gears and other parts that turn.

An adult must carefully supervise and facilitate a take-apart activity. Young children usually do not have the dexterity and small-motor skills to use tools and manipulate small pieces of machines and appliances safely. This activity is best done at a table with a small group of children.

Prep the take-apart machine ahead of time to ensure the activity will be successful. Check online for information about possible hazardous materials in the

item you are taking apart. Beware of electronic devices, such as TV sets, that may contain hazardous materials. A good resource for information about safely taking apart household items is the Instructables website: www.instructables.com/howto/take+apart.

As mentioned above, clocks and fans are ideal for a take-apart activity. Many electronic and mechanical toys also make for good take-aparts.

You will likely need a set of screwdrivers in different sizes to remove screws and open up the cover of the device or machine. Practice removing the cover ahead of time so you'll be ready to demonstrate this step for the children.

Prepare some small bins or trays for placing the smaller parts, hardware, and other components that you remove from the machine. The bins and trays can be used to pass the parts around the table so the children can look at them closely.

Before taking the machine apart, ask the children to make some guesses or predictions about what they will find inside. Then take off the cover of the device and look inside. Ask children what they see. If possible, document the process, along with their observations, using audio or video recordings and photos.

If possible, give children active roles in the take-apart process. They may be able to help you turn the screwdriver to loosen a screw or help gather bolts into a box.

Be sure to pass around the parts for children to look at closely. You may also want to provide magnifying glasses or flashlights to help children with their observations.

During and after the take-apart activity, ask open-ended questions such as these:

▶ What's inside a machine?

▶ What are the parts of a machine?

▶ How do we take things apart?

Afterward, look for opportunities for children to incorporate tools and hardware into their play. Many toy stores and school supply companies sell plastic or wooden nuts-and-bolts sets as well as tool sets.

Activity 1.8
Clay Robots

In this activity, children build their own robots out of clay or dough and use real metal parts to add features to their robots. Making clay robots is a safe way for children to enjoy a sensory experience with authentic hardware components.

This activity will challenge children to further explore the essential question "What is a robot?" Building robots out of clay and hardware also explores questions such as "What is the structure (shape and form) of a robot?" and "What are the parts of a robot?"

For this activity, you will need soft clay or dough and hardware, such as nuts, bolts, and washers.

Place hardware on a tray or on paper plates and invite children to incorporate the metal pieces into their clay robots. Often the children will use the hardware to create faces and other features on their robots. The children can save and take home their creations, or you could instruct the children, as part of the process, to take apart their creations and put the hardware back in the trays to be used again.

To extend and expand on children's ideas and creations, you can introduce other materials to incorporate. Here are some recommended items:

- toothpicks

- strings

- wire

- bottle caps

Activity 1.9
What Is Metal?

As you engage in conversations about machines and robots with children, they will likely make some observations about the colors and textures of the materials from which the devices are made. Some young children may already be familiar with the word "metal" and may know a little bit about what it means. They may know that metal can be a hard and shiny material, that it often appears silver or gray in color, or that most cars and trucks are made primarily out of metal.

In this activity, children explore the characteristics of metal and develop hands-on experience identifying objects made out of metal. As you explore the concept of metal with children, consider and discuss these big questions:

- ▷ What is metal?

- ▷ What is metal good for?

- ▷ Why would someone choose to make something out of metal?

- ▷ How is metal different from other materials, such as cloth or wood?

For this activity, you will need the following materials:

- a variety of metal objects found around school or home

- a basket or box for collecting things

- removable stickers or sticky notes

Begin by placing several metal items on a table. Ask children to explore the items and think about what all these things have in common. Items might include a spoon, a pan, a piece of foil, or a toy car made out of metal. Ask, "How are all these things the same?"

After the children have had an opportunity to touch and talk about the metal objects, ask the children if they have any ideas about what all the objects have in common. For very young children (three or four years old), who might not yet be familiar with the word "metal," you could guide the children to notice the silver color as something the items have in common. Children who are a bit older may be able to identify the common material and use the word "metal" without prompting. Take your time, listen to the children, and see how the conversation develops.

Once children have identified the common material as metal, invite them to hunt for metal in the classroom or school environment. You could give them a box or basket to collect metal things, or they could attach a sticker or sticky note to larger items or items like doorknobs that are attached to other things. Take photos or make lists to document children's discoveries.

The children's conversations around the question "Is this metal?" will lead naturally to some discussion of the characteristics of metal. Initially children may be focused solely on color; they may believe that all silver things are metal or that metal is always silver. Additional experiences, conversations, and observations will help challenge and expand children's thinking. Some children will be able to begin noticing other characteristics, such as a shiny surface. This activity is a good introduction to the next activity, which involves using magnets to help identify what is metal and what is not.

Activity 1.10
Magnets—Is It Metal?

Magnets are fascinating tools. Magnets are made out of metal, and magnets are attracted to certain kinds of metal. Many young children have played with magnetic toys, such as magnetic tiles, but they may not have been aware that the plastic pieces contain magnets that stick to one another. In many magnetic construction toys, the magnets are hidden or difficult to see. Children may not be aware that the toys have magnets inside of them. For this activity, the best type of magnet to use is a large, strong horseshoe or bar magnet. These large magnets, which are not connected to or part of a toy or construction set, allow children to see and explore the specific characteristics of magnets. You will also need different kinds of small objects, some metal and some not, as well as two bins or baskets. (Label the containers with words or symbols to designate "metal" and "not metal.")

As you invite the children to explore the magnets, consider and discuss these big questions:

▶ What is metal?

▶ What is a magnet?

▶ How do magnets interact with metal?

This activity works well when you introduce the materials and demonstrate the activity in a large group, and then make the materials available for children to use on their own in a learning center. Introduce this activity to children in a large group by asking the children, "What is metal?" Document their answers on a chart or list. Then ask, "How do you know if something is metal or not?"

Show children a magnet and say, "I have a tool that will help us figure out if something is metal. It's called a magnet." Demonstrate how a magnet will attract or stick to something that is metal. Invite children to use the magnets to help them figure out which items are metal and which are not.

A related activity that children may enjoy is hiding or burying metal items in a bin of rice or other loose material and using magnets to find the items.

Depending on what objects you use for these activities, the children may discover that a magnet will not attract some types of metal, such as copper pennies. This discovery can lead to a conversation about different kinds of metals. Magnets are attracted to metals like iron and nickel. Magnets are not attracted to metals like copper, silver, or aluminum.

Activity 1.11
Build with "Metal" Blocks

Cooking foil is a wonderful classroom material for young children because it is flexible. Children can bend and mold foil into different shapes. Most cooking foil is made out of aluminum, which is not attracted to magnets.

In this activity, you will observe what happens when you cover wooden blocks in foil and invite children to construct "metal" buildings and machines. Playing with foil-covered blocks allows children to continue to explore the big question "What is metal?" Here are other big questions to consider and discuss:

▶ What is metal?

▶ What is wood?

▶ How are wood and metal different?
   How are they the same?

Introduce this activity to the whole group, then make the materials available in the block area during free play. You will need at least one roll of cooking foil, as well as a set of wooden blocks. (Standard unit blocks work best.)

To prepare, cover some wooden unit blocks with foil ahead of time. Then show children the blocks and ask, "How are these different from the blocks you know?

What are they made out of?" Then invite the children to build and experiment with the foil-covered blocks.

Observe the children's play. It may be interesting to note if the foil influences the ways in which the children build and play with blocks. Are the children more likely to build machines or robots when the blocks are shiny and smooth like metal?

During or after block play, ask the children, "Which is better for building? Metal or wood? Why do you think so?"

As an extension of this activity, the children may be interested in covering some of the blocks with foil themselves. Or they may want to use foil in other ways, to bend and shape and make things.

As another extension activity, invite children to compare similar items made out of wood and metal side by side, such as a wooden spoon and a metal spoon. Encourage children to touch and hold the items and compare how they feel in their hands. Which one feels smoother? Which one feels heavier? Which spoon would you rather use to eat your dinner, and why?

Activity 1.12
Robots in Real Life

Up to this point, you and the children have probably been using the words "robot" and "machine" interchangeably. Now it's time to offer an activity that will expose children to the idea that a robot is not an ordinary machine. It is programmable. A robot has a brain called a computer (or computer chip, known technically as an integrated circuit). People program a robot by giving it commands. We tell robots what to do.

In this activity, you will introduce children to a real robot, a machine with an operating system (a computer) that runs it and tells it what to do. A smartphone, an ATM, and a Roomba (robotic vacuum cleaner) are a few examples that are likely to be present already in the lives of young children.

A Roomba is an especially good example of a real robot because it not only has a computer chip or circuit board, but it also moves around. Movement, as you may have observed during some of the previous activities, such as activity 1.5 (Robot Dance Party) is an essential characteristic of a robot.

This activity will inspire conversations around many of the big questions about robots:

▸ What is a robot?

▸ What can a robot do?

▸ What robots do you know?

▸ Do families need robots? Why or why not?

This activity works best as a planned group activity, introduced when you see that children are noticing and thinking about the ways we program robots. You will need a device that demonstrates many, if not all, of the essential characteristics of a robot: it is programmable (has a computer or computer chip); it has a practical function (provides some kind of helpful service to people); and it performs some kind of action or movement (or makes a sound). The easiest example to find within your reach is probably a smartphone or tablet, though a device that moves would be even better. Perhaps there is an ATM within walking distance; the children will observe how the machine has mechanisms for reading a card and dispensing cash. Or perhaps you have access to a Roomba or another programmable household device.

To begin, gather the children and tell them that you have a robot you'd like them to meet. Show them the device you have chosen for the activity. Demonstrate how it works. If children say, "That's not a robot," ask them, "Why isn't this a robot?" If possible, make the device talk or perform an action in response to a command. Use the word "command" frequently as you explain how the device works. This is an important vocabulary word for children to learn as they grow to understand that programming a robot means that we create a command that tells it what to do. Suggest, "Let's tell this robot what to do," and ask, "What command can we give this robot?" Then invite children to draw or make a model of the robot out of clay. Invite the children to dictate a description of the robot.

Activity 1.13
Be the Boss of a Robot

To deepen and clarify children's understanding of how we program robots, revisit the picture book described in activity 1.6, *Me and My Robot* by Tracey West. Revisiting this story after children have some experience observing and experiencing the concept of commands can lead to some fruitful discussion of the big question "How do we tell robots what to do?"

Read the story aloud, then invite the children to act out the story, taking on the roles of the boy, Reese; his robot, Robot; and Reese's friend Lucy. Other children can play the roles of the animals in the story: the dog, some ants, a squirrel, a rabbit, and, of course, the kitten. Read the story again and have the story actors move and speak the dialogue as best they can.

Afterward, ask the children, "Who was in charge of the robot? Who told the robot what to do?" Discuss how Reese's robot is similar to the real robot you observed in the previous activity. A robot is something you command.

Next, children may enjoy playing a robot version of the game Simon Says. Have the children be the robots, and you, as Simon, be the programmer. Use the term "command" to describe the instructions that Simon gives during the game. Say, for example, "Robots, here is your first command. Simon says put your hands on your head."

Activity 1.14
Is This a Robot?

In this activity, you will present children with a variety of objects. Each one demonstrates at least one characteristic of a robot. You will ask the children, "Is this a robot? Why or why not?" There are no right or wrong answers. The conversations and explorations will develop children's critical thinking skills as they evaluate and compare the objects and consider many of the most important foundational characteristics of robots. This activity will address the following big questions:

- What is a robot?
- What is a machine?
- What is a computer?
- What's the difference between a machine and a robot?
- Are all machines robots? Are all robots machines?
- What's the difference between a robot and a computer?

You will need a variety of objects, each one demonstrating a characteristic of a robot. Here is a suggested combination:

- something that looks like a robot but doesn't actually work, such as a wooden or rubber robot toy or a picture of a robot

- a simple machine—something that serves a purpose but is not programmable, such as a real or toy clock, a pencil sharpener, a stapler, or a coffeemaker

- something that is programmable, such as a computer, smartphone, or tablet (I use an old, broken smartphone for this activity so I can let children play with it and not worry that it will be damaged.)

- something that looks like a part of a robot, such as a plastic toy robot hand or toy grabber

This activity works well as a morning provocation, an activity presented to children as they are arriving in the classroom. You can invite children to touch and play with the objects and engage in conversations about what is a robot and what is not. For each item, ask the children, "Is this a robot?" Ask them to explain their thinking. Document children's responses by making an audio or video recording or taking notes.

Based on the children's ideas, create a documentation board or poster in response to the question "What is a robot?" Or, if you have already started this documentation (as suggested in activity 1.6), use this opportunity to revisit and revise your classroom definition of the word "robot."

Here are some of the important ideas children may begin to develop:

▷ A robot is a machine. It's made out of parts. Some of the parts are metal.

▷ A robot is not a person. A robot moves, but it's not alive.

▷ A robot has a job to do. People make robots do things. People tell robots what to do. If you give a command to a robot, it will do what you want it to do.

Activity 1.15
Robot Dramatic Play

If you've been implementing some of the introductory activities in this book, reading stories about robots, and having exciting conversations about robots, the children may already be pretending to be robots as part of free play and outdoor play. In this activity, you and the children will make a simple robot costume out of foil and cardboard to use as a prop during pretend play.

Children can prepare the robot costume as a project in the art area, then use the box or boxes in the dramatic play area during free play. The suggested materials for this activity include the following:

● cardboard boxes large enough for children to wear as a costume (Cut holes in advance for children's head and arms if worn over the torso, or cut an opening for the child's face if worn as a helmet.)

● large roll of foil

● glue

● tape

● stickers

To begin, invite children to cover and decorate the boxes with foil and stickers. Guide the children to flatten the sheets of foil against the sides of the box or boxes and secure them with glue or tape. Use stickers or other craft items to make robot features, such as buttons or switches, nuts and bolts, or battery packs.

When the costumes are complete and the glue is dry, the children can take turns wearing the robot costumes and pretending to be robots. As children play, observe their actions, listen to their dialogue, and write down what you see and hear as a story. Begin with the phrase "Once there was a robot." Share the story with the children at group time.

An observed story based on children's pretend play might read something like this: "Once there was a robot named Elliot. He was friends with a kitten and a turtle. They lived in a cave and ate ice cream. Except robots don't eat ice cream. They eat rocks for their batteries. The robot never went to sleep. His eyes were always open."

Activity 1.16
Questions about Robots

The previous activities in this chapter have encouraged children to think about what they already know about robots and extend that knowledge through play, exploration, and stories. Children have only just begun a lifelong journey learning about technology. Before continuing with new activities, take a moment to ask the children what else they want to know about robots. Use these questions to guide your next steps. You could do this activity as a large group during story time or circle time, or in smaller groups or even individually during free play or meals.

Begin a list titled "Questions We Have about Robots." Encourage children to contribute their thoughts and ideas. Ask them, "What do you still want to know about robots?" and "What questions do you have about robots?"

Post the list on the wall of the classroom and add to it as new questions spontaneously arise. You may also want to invite family members to add to the list.

Use the list of questions to help you decide which activities to implement in chapters 2 through 5 of this book. Using an inquiry-based learning structure, the direction and topics of the curriculum are aligned with the children's interests and are responsive to the children's curiosity and questions.

2

How Do We Build Robots?

Thinking Like an Engineer

This chapter offers ideas and activities for introducing children to robot construction. It includes basic concepts related to mechanical engineering, spatial reasoning, physics, and design engineering.

Young children often have a keen interest in how things work. Through construction and deconstruction experiences, children learn how parts make up a whole. This is true of a simple wooden puzzle, and it's true of a complex robotic device. What makes a robot different from a wooden puzzle, however, is that a robot, like many other mechanical devices, moves and has power. Exploring motion and power is the focus of many of these activities.

Hexbugs: A Robot Case Study

In each of the next activities, we'll conduct a case study of one particular type of robotic toy. In my experience leading these activities with young children, I often have used robotic toys called Hexbugs. Hexbugs are bio-inspired robots. Many of the Hexbug robots are designed, built, and programmed to mimic creatures that exist in the living world. The Hexbug line of toys includes a variety of different kinds of creatures. The Nano is modeled after a common cockroach. There are also Hexbug spiders, larvae, and ants. Hexbug AquaBots are robots that can swim. Any robotic toy would work well for these first five activities in our robot case study, but these examples use Hexbugs because of the variety of types, sizes, and designs of the creatures. The simplest and smallest Hexbug toys, such as the Nano, are also less expensive than larger, more complex robotic toys currently on the market.

Activity 2.1
Robot Free Play

The first step in introducing young children to a new device or toy is simply to allow time and space for free play. Children will not be ready to discuss, observe, analyze, and reflect on how the devices work until they've had a chance to touch, manipulate, and play with these fascinating creatures. As mentioned earlier, the examples used in this activity are Hexbugs.

As children explore these toys, they can ponder the following big questions:

▶ What can robot toys do?

▶ How do they work?

▶ How do they move?

First, gather several robotic toys, enough for a small group of children to use together. Here are some recommended models of Hexbug toys (see www.hexbug .com):

- Hexbug Nano

- Hexbug Scarab

- Hexbug Fire Ant

And here are some other robotic toy options:

- WowWee robotic animals, cars, or dinosaurs (http://wowwee.com)

- Fisher-Price Bright Beats baby toys (www.fisher-price.com/en_US/baby /fpbaby/bright-beats/index.html)

Most young children are fascinated by robotic toys and are eager to play with them. When you first introduce robotic toys to young children, you may need to establish a plan for sharing the toys, perhaps including a sign-up sheet and a time limit for each child. Teacher supervision and support will help children understand that even the most durable electronic toys need careful handling. Establishing

some simple rules and developmentally appropriate expectations for the use of electronic toys now will help the children understand and enjoy using more sophisticated devices later.

Take note of children's questions and comments as they play with the robotic toys. What fascinates them most? Are they curious about how the devices work or how they're made? Pay careful attention to comments on how the devices move and any use of words related to the device's power source, such as "power," "battery," "strong," or "fast." You'll be able to build on these comments and questions in the next activities.

Activity 2.2
Real or Robot?

This activity challenges children to think about how robots are similar to and different from real, living things. Hexbug insects work well for this activity because many are bio-inspired robots, made to look like real insects and engineered to move like real insects.

As children explore these toys, they can ponder the following big questions:

▶ How is a robot like a living thing?

▶ How is a robot different from a living thing?

▶ How can we know what is alive and what is not alive?

For this activity, you'll need the following materials:

● robotic toys, such as Hexbugs

● images, videos, or examples of the living creatures on which the robotic toys are modeled (For insects, such as ants or cockroaches, you can purchase real bugs preserved in plastic from school supply companies such as Celestron: www.celestron.com/browse-shop/microscopes/microscope-accessories /other-microscope-accessories.)

Show the children an image, video, or example of a living creature that is similar to the robotic toy. For example, the Hexbug Nano is designed to look and move like a cockroach. For comparison, you could show the children a video of a cockroach, such as www.youtube.com/watch?v=iowSdSCSUwY.

After viewing the video or image, invite the children to observe how the robotic toy looks and moves. Invite the children to move their own bodies in ways that imitate the robots. Discuss the similarities and differences between the living creature and the robot. How is this robot similar to the living thing? How is this robot different from the living thing? Take note of the children's ideas and observations.

Some children may enjoy drawing a picture of the robot and a picture of the living creature. The process of drawing a picture will help children observe and think about the specific characteristics and details. Some children may also enjoy making clay models of the robots and the creatures.

Activity 2.3
Compare Robot to Robot

For this activity, you will need two different kinds of robotic toys. The purpose of this activity is to draw children's attention to the different structures and designs of robots and challenge children to make observations, develop ideas, and draw some initial conclusions about how robots are made and how the form or structure of the robot influences how the robot moves.

As children explore these toys, they can ponder the following big questions:

▸ How are these two robots different from each other?

▸ What do these robots have in common?

As children play with the robots side by side, discuss the ways in which the robots are similar and the ways in which they are different. Ask open-ended questions that will draw children's attention to the design, structure, and movement of the robots:

▸ What do you notice about how these robots look?

▸ Are they the same size? Or is one bigger and one smaller?

▸ What do you notice about how these robots move?

▸ Does one move faster than the other? Which one is faster?

▸ What do you notice about the pieces and parts of these robots and how the pieces are put together?

As children notice details about how the robots look and how they are made, some of the children may comment on the materials used to make the robots. If a robotic toy has any metal parts, you may want to connect these observations and experiences to activities 1.9, 1.10, and 1.11 in the previous chapter.

Activity 2.4
Robot Hospital

Most robotic toys, such as Hexbugs, will eventually malfunction in some way. The battery will run out of power, or a part will loosen, and suddenly the toy no longer works or doesn't work as well as it once did. Fortunately, these malfunctions can become teachable moments in the classroom.

When children create a robot hospital for malfunctioning robots, they can ponder the following big questions:

▶ Why do robots sometimes stop working?

▶ How do we fix broken robots?

For this activity, you'll need the following materials:

● a broken robotic toy

● extra batteries

● screwdrivers of various sizes

When a robotic toy stops working properly, invite the children to create a robot hospital. The children may enjoy creating a welcoming hospital-like environment that's similar to a human hospital, with a soft blanket or bed on which the robot can rest. The children may also enjoy using dramatic play props, such a doctor's coat and toy stethoscope, to pretend that they are taking care of the broken robot as a doctor would care for a patient in a hospital.

Start a conversation with the children about what they think is wrong with the robot. Some children might have ideas that are fanciful or based on a personification of the robot, such as "The robot has the flu" or "The robot has a broken heart." Some children might have ideas that are more accurate, based on their observations and experiences with machines and robots, such as "It needs a new battery" or "The wires might be loose."

With any battery-powered toy, a weak or dead battery is often the cause of a malfunction. If you have extra batteries that are the right size for this particular robotic toy, suggest that changing the battery is an option, and invite the children to help you try to fix the toy. In most cases, a Phillips screwdriver will be the only equipment you need to change the battery. The manufacturer's website may provide specific details about what type of battery is needed and how to change it. Young children will probably not yet have the dexterity to assist with the tools, but you can give them turns to help by holding a flashlight or handing off the tools while you or another adult changes the battery.

If changing the battery does not fix the toy, discuss with the children other ideas they may have for why the toy is not working. Brainstorm possibilities and make a list of the children's ideas. A related topic of discussion that might interest the children is whether a broken robot is still fun to play with and whether it still has any value. Sometimes children have very interesting opinions and responses to such questions and enjoy debating the pros and cons of keeping a broken toy.

Activity 2.5
Robot Take-Aparts

If one of your robotic toys is broken, and changing the battery does not get it running again, the next step could be to take the device apart. Opening up the device and examining the inside can be an educational experience for all involved. The process may or may not reveal why the device stopped working. Regardless, children will learn firsthand about the parts and pieces of a robot.

As children take apart a robot, they can ponder the following big questions:

▸ What's inside a robot?

▸ How do robots work?

▸ What are the parts of a robot, and how do they fit together?

For this activity, you'll need a broken robotic toy. You'll also need a set of screwdrivers and other basic tools.

Taking apart any toy or electronic device requires direct adult supervision. In fact, the adult's role is to lead and demonstrate the process. The children are primarily observers in this process.

The first challenge in taking apart a toy is removing the cover or opening up the case. High-quality toys are very durable. They're designed and built to prevent children from accidentally or intentionally taking them apart. You may need to carefully study the device before you can determine the best course of action.

Often, the first step is opening up the battery case. This opening may be more obvious than other openings, especially if this is a toy that regularly requires fresh batteries.

After you've removed the battery, additional openings or screws that you could not see from the outside may become visible. Once the case or cover is open, here are some of the parts or components you might see:

Motor A typical toy motor looks like a silver metal cylinder. You may be able to see a prong or axle sticking out from one end of the cylinder. There may also be two wires attached to the motor. Often, one wire is blue and the other is red.

Circuit board A circuit board supports and connects the electronic components of the toy. It has a flat base called a substrate that's often made of fiberglass. This base is covered with copper layers or lines and a thin top layer called solder mask, which is usually green in color. The circuit board may have symbols or numbers printed on it (Hord, accessed 2017).

Speakers or lightbulbs If the toy makes sounds or lights up, you may be able to see small speakers or lightbulbs. There will be wires connecting the speakers and lightbulbs to the other components.

Hardware Look for hardware that supports the movement of the device. You may see wheels, joints, hinges, or screws.

As you progress through the take-apart process, pause as each new piece is exposed and let each child view the device. Ask discussion questions:

▶ What parts do you see?

▶ What is the color, shape, or size of that part?

▶ What do you think is the function of that part? What does it do?

▶ What materials do you think that part is made of? Do you think it's made of metal?

▷ Have you ever seen anything like this before?

▷ Does this part or piece remind you of anything else you've seen before?

You may come across an obvious, visible problem, such as a cracked piece or a frayed wire, that you can identify as the cause of the malfunction. Even if you can't identify the problem, the children will learn from seeing the parts inside the toy and identifying the characteristics of these parts.

Research more information about the names, functions, and structures of various parts. One helpful resource may be the children's families. Some family members may have experience with electronic devices in their professional roles, through hobbies, or simply from their own experience building and fixing things at home. Help the children think of questions they can ask their families to gather more information. You may want to send a note home about this or post a notice in the classroom.

Activity 2.6
Electron Game

The part of a toy that many children may be able to identify and recognize is the battery. So many familiar household devices depend on batteries for power that even very young children have probably heard the word "battery" before and have seen adults change or charge batteries.

Batteries are not safe for children to touch and play with, because batteries contain chemicals and because they create an electrical charge. But children may be curious about how batteries work. This activity provides children with a kinesthetic explanation of how electrons flow through a circuit from one battery terminal to the other.

As children play the electron game, they can ponder the following big questions:

▷ What is a battery?

▷ How is it made?

▷ How does it work?

For this activity, you will need pictures of batteries in different shapes and sizes.

In a small group, show children some images of batteries. Ask children to talk about what they see in the pictures. Explain that a battery is a container full of chemicals. Chemicals are powerful materials. Batteries have two terminals, or points. One is positive and one is negative. The battery's power comes from tiny particles called electrons. The electrons flow from one terminal to the other as fast as they can, over a wire or other connection.

To play a group electron game, you'll need plenty of space, such as a playground or gym. Explain to the children that you are all going to pretend to be a giant battery together. Have the children form a circle and hold hands. Tell the children that the circle they have formed is a circuit, and that the electrons can now travel along the circle or circuit. To demonstrate the way an electron can travel along a circuit, have the children send a gentle hand squeeze from one friend to another, all around the circle. Some children may have played a "friendship squeeze" game like this before, but in this case the point of the game is to show how a complete and connected circle or circuit is necessary for an electron to move and carry electricity.

Next, invite one of the children to come into the middle of the circle to play the role of a dancing electron. This part of the game is similar to a traditional freeze dance game. The electron in the middle can move around and dance in any chosen way, but only when the circuit is fully connected. The child playing the role of the electron has to keep an eye on the circle and notice when the circuit becomes broken. The teacher could play the role of a circuit breaker, or a child could be assigned as a circuit breaker. Direct the children to join hands, and when the circuit is complete invite the "electron" to move. After a minute or two, the "circuit breaker" should let go of one or both hands and "break" the circle. At that moment, the "electron" must freeze. Practice this several times, rotating the roles of the electron and the circuit breaker. If your group enjoys the game and is ready for an additional challenge, the children in the circuit could also move, by all rotating in one direction, while the electron is dancing in the center. Again, the electron in the middle must freeze each time the circuit is broken.

A discussion of batteries and how they work may naturally lead to more questions about power, what it is, and where it comes from. The next activity, 2.7, features these ideas.

Power Conversations

As children learn more about how batteries provide power, they may become more curious about other sources of power. They may ask the following big questions:

▷ What is power?

▷ What is energy?

▷ Where do power and energy come from?

▷ What is electricity?

When conversations about power arise, ask questions that will challenge children to think about other machines and devices in their environment and what other sources of power might exist besides batteries. For example, you could spark a new conversation by demonstrating how you use a switch to turn on a light or how you plug a computer into an outlet. Ask the children, "Where do you think this light gets its power? Where do you think this computer gets its power?"

Some children may already know the word "electricity." You can explain that electric energy travels through wires, just like the power from a battery can travel through wires. A battery is a small container that stores electricity.

Ask children, "What else needs power or energy?" Some children may suggest vehicles, like cars or trucks. Some children may suggest people and animals. These ideas can open up new conversations about other sources of energy, such as fuel or food.

A discussion of power and energy among young children can sometimes lead to ideas about superpowers or superheroes. Don't worry if children's ideas about power are based on fantasy rather than fact. Explore these ideas with the same seriousness and interest as you would approach a discussion of batteries and electricity. Ask open-ended questions, such as "What kind of power do you wish you had?"

Activity 2.8
Things That Light Up

Flashlights, projectors, and things that light up make energy visible in exciting ways. Playing with light, color, and shadow is a tangible way for children to experiment with sources of power and energy. As children do so, they can ponder the following big questions:

▷ Where does light come from?

▷ What makes things light up?

▷ What can we do with light?

For this activity, you will need a variety of things that light up, such as the following:

● flashlights

● a projector

● a light table

● light-up toys, such as a Lite Brite or glow sticks

During free play at learning centers, provide things that light up as one option for open-ended play. Use a tent or a separate, darkened space to help the light of the toys or devices be more visible.

Observe children's play and listen to their conversations about light. During or after play, ask children open-ended questions that will prompt them to make connections with what they are learning about power and energy:

▷ Where does the light come from?

▷ How does the light work?

▷ What kind of power does the light need in order to shine?

▷ Why is some light brighter than other lights? What makes it so bright?

Take note of children's comments and ideas. Use this information to help you shape your decisions about next steps in your curriculum.

Activity 2.9
Circuit Sets

If the children continue to demonstrate an interest in learning more about power, energy, and electricity, you might offer them educational toys made specifically for exploring these concepts. As children play with circuit sets, they can ponder the following big questions:

▶ How does electricity work?

▶ What can we do with electricity?

▶ How do we make things that will really work?

If your budget allows the purchase of specialized educational materials, several sets on the market allow children to build their own simple circuits:

Snap Circuits Components snap together on a plastic frame. Each component contains a separate function, such as a switch or a light. Each piece is numbered and color-coded. Just follow the pictures in the manual to create specific projects, such as a doorbell or light. The recommended age for Snap Circuits is eight years and older, but younger children could use them with guidance and supervision. (www.snapcircuits.net)

MakerBloks MakerBloks are similar to Snap Circuits but are geared toward a younger age group. Each block contains a magnet, so the blocks can connect easily to other blocks and form a fully functioning circuit. For example, children can connect a battery block to an LED block to create a light. (https://makerbloks.com/#/explore)

littleBits littleBits building blocks are magnetic, like MakerBloks, but are smaller in size, like Snap Circuits. The littleBits website includes STEM lesson plans for teachers. (http://littlebits.cc)

Squishy Circuits Squishy Circuits use playdough to teach the basics of electrical circuits. The set includes recipes for two kinds of dough: one that is conductive (electricity flows through it) and one that is insulating (electricity cannot flow through it). The set also includes LED lights and a battery pack. (https://squishycircuits.com)

Activity 2.10
Simple Machines

The next seven activities in this chapter demonstrate concepts of physical science that are called simple machines. Simple machines include the following:

- inclined plane, also known as a ramp

- wedge, a tool used to separate, such as a knife, ax, or needle

- lever, a pole, rod, or plank used to lift something, such as a crowbar

- screw, as found on a jar lid, drill, or lightbulb

- pulley, a wheel combined with a rope or cord that can be used to lift objects up and down

- wheel and axle, one of the most important inventions in the history of the world

A simple machine uses a single applied force to do work against a single load force. Work is the amount of energy needed to move an object. To move the object farther, you need to do more work (Idaho Public Television, accessed 2014).

It's neither necessary nor developmentally appropriate to teach children the names and definitions of simple machines, but it is helpful for teachers to understand that these devices are the building blocks of mechanical engineering. Teachers need to know that children benefit from hands-on experimentation with simple machines. Through this experimentation, they begin developing an understanding of how things move when we apply force or energy.

As early childhood educators, we can provide the materials and learning environments where these explorations can take place. We can ask questions and make comments that help children become good observers and testers of physical science phenomena.

For inspiration in helping children observe the movement of objects, we can turn to Friedrich Froebel, the "father of kindergarten." In the 1800s, Froebel developed a sequence of learning tools he called "gifts" for use in early childhood classrooms. The first gift is a simple ball. Norman Brosterman (1997, 42) writes in *Inventing Kindergarten*, a comprehensive history of Froebel's work creating the first kindergarten, "Perfect in form, the ball, or sphere, was the practical expression of stability and the material expression of motion. By grasping, rolling, dropping, hiding, and swinging the ball, the child gained intuitive and experiential knowledge of object, space, time, color, movement, attraction, union, independence, and gravity." A simple ball has just as much to teach us in the twenty-first century. These same concepts of motion—how a three-dimensional sphere moves through space and down to Earth—are relevant foundational concepts for all STEM learning.

As children play with a ball, they can explore the following big questions:

▸ How do things move?

▸ Why do things move?

▸ What happens when we throw a ball?

▸ What happens when we roll a ball?

▸ How does the movement of our arm affect the movement of the ball?

You can do this activity with a large group, small group, or with just one child. It involves playing a simple game of catch, either throwing or rolling a ball back and forth, in a circle with a group of children or across from a single child. What makes this activity meaningful is the way you draw children's attention to the movement of the ball.

As you throw the ball, ask, "How does the ball move? Does it go up? Does it go down? Does it travel in a straight line? What happens when I throw hard? What happens when I throw gently?"

Before, during, or after you throw the ball back and forth, ask children to draw a line on a piece of paper or a whiteboard to show how a ball travels through the air. You may notice that once children have watched the ball carefully, they will change the way they draw the lines. The children may also enjoy watching and discussing this video showing a robot that can catch a ball: www.youtube.com /watch?v=83eGcht7IiI.

Activity 2.11
Daisy's Wild Ride

Finding picture books that demonstrate physics and engineering concepts can be challenging. Often children's science books are either too high-level in content, or the story does not represent the science concepts accurately. One rare exception is *Daisy's Wild Ride* by Bob Graham. In this story, a child sends her pet pig, Daisy, down a hill in a wagon. The wagon hits a bump and stops, but the force of the downhill motion propels Daisy forward until she lands (happily) in a puddle of mud. The story beautifully demonstrates Newton's first law of motion: an object in motion will continue in motion with the same speed in the same direction unless acted upon by an unbalanced force. In Daisy's case, the unbalanced force is the mud puddle. For young children, the important idea is recognizing that often, for something to stop moving, something else must get in its way.

Activity 2.12
Ramps

It's easy to find an example of one simple machine, the inclined plane, in an early childhood classroom. Just look in the block corner. A typical set of unit blocks includes half-unit triangles, quarter-unit triangles, and unit-block ramps.

As children play with these blocks, they can ponder the following big questions:

▸ What is a ramp?

▸ How do we use ramps?

▶ Are all ramps the same?

▶ If not, what are some of the differences?

▶ How does the shape of the ramp affect the way a car or ball rolls?

In a small group of children, take one block in each shape—the half-unit triangle, the quarter-unit triangle, and the unit-block ramp—and set them down on the floor or on a tabletop. Ask the children to describe what they see. You may want to document their answers on paper or in an audio or video recording. Ask children open-ended questions to help them notice the details in size and shape, such as "How are these blocks the same? How are they different?"

Invite the children to play with the blocks by rolling a toy car down each ramp. You may want to add some other blocks to help build a platform or road at the top and bottom of the ramp. Ask children to evaluate the way each type of ramp functions when a car is rolling down it: "If you were driving this car, which ramp would you want to drive on? Why?"

During this discussion, children may talk about the steepness of the ramps. They may not yet have the words to describe what they see, and will likely use gestures to demonstrate the concept. If they are curious and engaged in the activity, teach them the word "steep." Show them that the quarter-unit triangles are very steep, the ramps are not very steep, and the half-unit triangles are in between. Some children may be ready to learn the word "angle" as well. You can draw the angle of each ramp on a piece of paper by laying the block on the page and tracing the angle of the ramp. For children who are ready for an advanced challenge, show them how to use a protractor to measure the angle.

Activity 2.13
Marble Runs

Marble runs are construction toys that allow children to build a path for a marble to travel through tubes and holes. Many commercial marble run sets are available through toy stores and school supply catalogs. Marble runs are wonderful toys that provide a fun, hands-on experience with Newton's laws of motion.

I also recommend the National Association for the Education of Young Children (NAEYC) publication *Ramps and Pathways: A Constructivist Approach to Physics with Young Children* by Rheta DeVries and Christina Sales. This book provides many exciting ideas for expanding children's play and STEM learning through the use of marble runs made out of cove molding, unit blocks, and a variety of other novel and open-ended materials. DeVries and Sales also present a detailed and cogent description of constructivist physical science concepts and teaching strategies. (See also Betty Zan and Rosemary Geiken's excellent article on the same topic at www.naeyc.org/files/naeyc/Ramps_Pathways.pdf.)

Activity 2.14
Wheels

Most young children enjoy playing with wheeled toys such as cars, trucks, and trains. In most high-quality early childhood classrooms, children have opportunities to play with wheeled toys every day, indoors and out. Sometimes children develop the misconception that wheeled toys are for boys, not girls, so make sure the girls in your classroom have plenty of opportunities to play with wheeled toys too.

Here are a few suggestions for extending children's learning during play with wheels:

Ask thought-provoking questions about wheels: "What is a wheel? Why do we need wheels? How do wheels work?"

Compare wheels: Find a toy with big wheels and a toy with small wheels and ask children to compare them side by side. Ask children to predict which toy will move faster—the one with the big wheels or the one with the smaller wheels. Then test the toys in a race to see if their predictions were correct.

Learn from broken toys: If a wheeled toy happens to break, use this event as a teachable moment. A broken toy may now have the pieces exposed, allowing the children to better see and understand how an axle connects two wheels.

Activity 2.15
Study a Bicycle

The Reggio Emilia schools in Italy are regarded as an international model for a project approach to early childhood education. The Reggio Emilia teachers frequently use bicycles in their classrooms to inspire conversations about how things work. In fact, the entire city of Reggio Emilia, Italy, engaged in an intergenerational project in which citizens of every age were invited to create drawings and other presentations of an ordinary bicycle (Ceppi et al. 2014).

Bring a bicycle into your classroom and observe the children's reactions. The conversations could spark many interesting projects and representations.

For more information about the Reggio Emilia perspective and the project approach, see Peggy Martalock's article "What Is a Wheel?" at www.southernearly childhood.org/upload/pdf/Dimensions_Vol40_3_Martalock.pdf.

Activity 2.16
Gears

Gears are a special kind of wheel. A gear is a wheel with teeth all around its rim. The teeth mesh together with the teeth on another gear. When one gear moves, its teeth push on the teeth of the other gear and make the gear turn (LA Tech STEP 2007).

As children play with toy gear sets in this activity, they can ponder the following big questions:

▶ What is a gear?

▶ How do gears work?

▶ What can we make with gears?

Many early childhood classrooms include plastic gear sets as a play option. Many school supply stores advertise gears as a valuable STEM teaching tool. (For example, see www.learningresources.com/category/brand/gears-gears-gears.do.) Yet I've observed that in many classrooms, children rarely choose the gear sets. My experience is that children as young as three, four, and even five years old often need some support and guidance to learn how to use gears in a satisfying way. Without guidance, children are likely to use the gears as simple wheels. They may construct a car that rolls on four gears as wheels, or they may place the gears on a pegboard in a pleasing pattern or tower. But they don't always take advantage of the teeth on the gears and place the gears close enough together so that the movement of one gear will turn another gear.

I recommend that you give children many opportunities to play with gears in whatever way they choose. But if you observe that children quickly lose interest in the gears or that their play doesn't utilize the gears' teeth and their unique function and power, take a moment to direct the children's attention to the gear structure and gently suggest some options for interesting construction projects.

In a small group, place a gear next to an ordinary wheel and ask children to compare the two kinds of wheels. Hold up the gear and ask, "What's special about this wheel?" Show the children how one gear can be placed next to another. Explain and demonstrate that a gear is a wheel with teeth, bumps that stick out all

around the rim of the wheel. Gears can make things move. When a gear turns, its teeth can push on the teeth of another gear.

Many machines and vehicles have gears, but often the gears are hidden inside the machine, where children cannot see them. One notable exception to this is a penny press. Many children have seen a penny press machine at tourist attractions or amusement parks. You put a penny in, pay an additional fee, and then you can turn a handle and watch the big gears turn inside the machine. The turning gears push the penny press together, and the result is a penny printed with a design related to the park or tourist attraction. For example, here's an image of the inside of a penny press at a science museum.

As you discuss the uses of gears in the real world, ask children if they have ever pressed a penny when they were on vacation or visiting a special place. For many children, this question will provide a meaningful connection to the real-life applications of gears. Invite the children to use the toy gears to create a model of a penny press.

Activity 2.17

Design Thinking

The term "design thinking" has gained popularity in industry, arts, and education. It describes a creative process that emphasizes experimentation and collaboration (Chao 2015). While there's no single definition of a design thinking process, it usually involves the following steps:

- Ask a question.

- Imagine a solution.

- Make a plan.

- Create something.

- Test it out and seek feedback.

- Improve it.

- Share it with others.

The design thinking process is circular, not linear; it never ends. Design thinking allows for endless iterations and innovation (EIE, accessed 2017).

What does design thinking have to do with early childhood education? How is design thinking relevant to our work with young children?

I think there are many elements of play that are already aligned with design thinking. I also believe that the most important idea from design thinking that can be applied to early childhood education is the circular process. We are all works in progress, and the children are continually learning, testing, improving.

In practice, I have one key suggestion for teachers for nurturing design thinking in your classroom: don't clean up. Or at least clean up less. Look for opportunities to allow children to revisit their projects over the course of many different play sessions. Whether children are building with blocks, painting on an easel, poking toothpicks into a ball of clay, or building a robot out of wire and bottle caps, try to find a protected space where the children can leave the work and come back to it again later. The passage of time allows children to reflect and reconsider, to incorporate new ideas, and to add new collaborators to the process.

Activity 2.18
The Most Magnificent Thing

You wouldn't send preschoolers to Stanford University's Institute of Design to learn design thinking, but you could read them Ashley Spires's 2014 picture book, *The Most Magnificent Thing.* This story of a little girl who wants to invent a contraption out of spare parts, a "most magnificent thing," is a wonderful demonstration of a design thinking process from a child's point of view. The young protagonist imagines and plans, then creates half a dozen iterations of her contraption. But none of them comes close to the vision in her head. She grows frustrated and almost gives up, but with the support of her neighbors and friends, she is able to make a fresh start and finally finish the project to her satisfaction. This book is a must-read for any classroom that values innovation and creativity.

Activity 2.19
Kinesthetic Machine—Car Wash

Visiting a drive-through car wash is an experience that many young children have shared with their families. Even children who have not seen a car wash before understand that cars get dirty and need to be washed. How cars get washed makes a rich topic of study and discussion among children. It also offers a meaningful connection between families' ordinary experiences and the design and function of machines and robots.

As children explore the idea of a car wash, they can ponder the following big questions:

- ▶ How do cars get dirty? How do they get clean?

- ▶ How does a car wash work?

- ▶ What kinds of machines are in a car wash?

Discuss the parts of a car wash or read a picture book about a car wash, such as *Car Wash* by Sandra Steen and Susan Steen. Then invite the children to act out the motions of the different machines in a car wash. Some of the children will be machines or robots, and some of the children will be cars going through the car wash.

Line up the children who will be the machines and assign them roles. Have the children make suggestions and demonstrate how they will move to dramatize the different machine functions, such as sprayer, soaper, scrubber, and dryer. Then have the rest of the children take turns pretending to be cars that drive through the car wash. The "cars" can crawl along the floor next to the machines.

Here are some other car wash picture books to try:

- *The Scrubbly-Bubbly Car Wash* by Irene O'Garden
- *Car Wash Kid* by Cathy Goldberg Fishman
- *Curious George Car Wash* by Margaret Rey and H. A. Rey
- *Dad's Car Wash* by Harry A. Sutherland
- *Henry Helps Wash the Car* by Beth Bracken
- *Isabel's Car Wa$h* by Sheila Bair

Activity 2.20
Water Table Car Wash

Extend the exploration and discussion of car washing machines by creating a miniature car wash in the water table, using real soap and water to wash toy cars. Children can pretend that squirt bottles are spraying machines. After the toy cars are clean and removed from the water table, children can blow air through drinking straws to simulate the power dryers.

Activity 2.21
Car Wash with Blocks and Pipe Cleaners

Another way to extend learning in the car wash topic is to add cars and pipe cleaners (chenilles) to the block corner. Invite children to create a drive-through car wash for the toy cars. They can bend the flexible pipe cleaners into the shape of brushes, sprayers, dryers, and water pipes.

Children may also be interested in viewing a video that shows the machines in a drive-through car wash, such as this Science Channel video: www.youtube.com /watch?v=8s3FiQDUaUQ.

Activity 2.22
The Domino Effect

For many children, knocking down their block structure is just as much fun as building it. Why do children enjoy knocking things down? Perhaps they just like making a big noise. But maybe they also benefit from observing how objects move as they fall, how they bump into each other, and what they look like when they come to rest in a new position. This is another real-life demonstration of Newton's laws of motion in an early childhood classroom.

Children who enjoy knocking things down may enjoy the challenge of creating a line of dominoes and watching how knocking over one domino will cause a chain reaction, making the rest of them fall in a wave. Standard-size dominoes are small and may be difficult for young children to manipulate. Oversize dominoes are available for purchase from many school supply stores. You could also use standard unit blocks to create a domino effect.

Many entertaining and fascinating domino videos are available online, such as the following:

- a video showing a variety of colorful and creative domino tricks: www.youtube.com/watch?v=ARM42-eorzE

- a video of a domino demonstration at the Maryland Science Center: www.youtube.com/watch?v=L7AVoJTkvec

Activity 2.23
Rube Goldberg Contraption

Rube Goldberg was a cartoonist in the mid-1900s. He was famous for his drawings of imagined contraptions. Each contraption accomplished a simple task using a complex series of cause-and-effect machines. Today many artists, engineers, and designers enjoy creating their own Rube Goldberg machines as a playful way to learn and demonstrate concepts of motion, physics, and mechanical engineering. Here's an example of a Rube Goldberg contraption that was created for a commercial advertising GoldieBlox toys: www.youtube.com/watch?v=IIGyVa5Xftw.

Most young children do not yet have the skills, knowledge, and dexterity to create elaborate Rube Goldberg machines. But with some guidance, they could create contraptions that incorporate two or more of the activities and ideas already presented in this chapter. For example, your class could set up a chain reaction of dominoes activated by a car rolling down a ramp (a combination of activity 2.12 and 2.22). What other activities could you combine?

○────────────●

Activity 2.24
Troubleshooting with Rosie Revere

The activities and suggestions in this book emphasize the important role of making mistakes in learning the STEM concepts involved in robotics. Whether we call it troubleshooting, debugging, revising, or messing up, the ability to take a learning risk, to experiment, and then to observe, evaluate, and acknowledge where the results did not meet the expectations or vision for the task, is an essential part of STEM learning and design thinking.

The picture book *Rosie Revere, Engineer* by Andrea Beaty beautifully illustrates the value of making mistakes, learning from them, and then moving on. Keep this book handy and pull it out whenever a child needs encouragement to keep trying to overcome obstacles and frustrations. In the story, little Rosie loves inventing gizmos and gadgets, but she is overcome by doubt and disappointment when her newest invention, a cheese-copter, crashes. Her beloved aunt Rose praises her "brilliant first flop" and encourages her to keep improving her inventions, explaining that we can only fail when we stop trying new ideas.

Activity 2.25
Mistake Party

The best way to respond to mistakes is to celebrate them as learning opportunities. And the best way to celebrate any occasion is with a fun party. Why not throw a mistake party?

Begin a class log on a big piece of poster paper. Write down the most wonderful mistakes the children make and what they learned from these mistakes. The list might include things like these:

- Maria spilled her milk cup, learned not to fill it so high.

- James knocked over Peter's tower, learned to build a little farther away.

- Luna counted the spoons 1-3-2, learned to say 1-2-3.

Once you've collected a nice variety of mistakes, throw a mistake party with treats, music, and dancing. Invite the children's families to attend. Invite guests to tell about wonderful mistakes they made. Read *The Most Magnificent Thing* or *Rosie Revere, Engineer* (from activities 2.18 and 2.24). Above all, treat each mistake lightly, as a welcome bump along the road to discovery.

3

How Do We Tell Robots What to Do?

Developing Spatial Intelligence

The activities in this chapter focus on the actual coding, or programming, of robots. People tell robots what to do by creating commands represented by a code, or programming language. With many of the educational robots described in this chapter, such as the Bee-Bot, the programming language is simple. To program the Bee-Bot, young children push buttons labeled with simple symbols on its back. In this case, arrows pointing in the direction of travel represent the programming language. As children grow older and learn more about robots and computer science, they will have opportunities to learn more complex programming languages, such as Scratch, Java, or Python.

Many of the robotic devices and coding apps currently available for young children focus on teaching children how to navigate a grid. Imagine a checkerboard marked with evenly measured squares. A beginning experience in coding often involves figuring out how to move a robot forward one space on a grid or, in the case of a coding app such as Kodable or Lightbot, to move an animated character one space forward on a virtual game board.

Navigating a grid is just one kind of spatial skill. Spatial skill, also known as spatial reasoning or spatial intelligence, means figuring out how we move through space, how objects or shapes move or are positioned in space, and the relationships between different objects or positions in space. The term "space" means any area that exists—a tabletop, a room, a city, the world. Spatial reasoning skills allow us to read maps, diagrams, charts, and graphs (Kris 2015).

Young children develop spatial reasoning skills and spatial intelligence through play using blocks, puzzles, and board games. They also develop these skills through drawing and three-dimensional art experiences, and by moving their bodies indoors and out. While many of the activities in this chapter involve specific robotic and coding devices and tools, the first four focus simply on the development of spatial reasoning skills and learning to navigate a grid using ordinary classroom materials.

Activity 3.1
Checkerboard Play

In this activity, children play freely with small blocks and toys on an ordinary checkerboard or on a paper grid. Children need not know how to play checkers, nor do they need to move their toys as they would in a game of checkers. You will probably notice, however, that when children play with toys on a checkerboard surface, they do tend to organize and move the toys in a linear fashion.

For this activity, you will need the following materials:

- checkerboard or a checkerboard-like grid drawn on paper or cardboard

- small blocks

- small toys, such as animal, dinosaur, or people figures

As children play with toys on a checkerboard, they can ponder the following big questions:

▶ How can we play with toys on a checkerboard?
How do we move the toys from space to space?

▶ How is playing on a checkerboard different from playing on a plain tabletop?

Another option is to cover the tabletop with oversize graph paper and allow the children to draw lines on the paper as they play. They may create lines that represent roads, landmarks, walls, or furniture. This spontaneous mapmaking process creates opportunities for deepening spatial reasoning skills.

Activity 3.2
The Big Grid

This activity brings the checkerboard grid outdoors and engages children in a kinesthetic, full-body learning experience. As children play on a giant grid, they can ponder the following big questions:

▸ What is a grid?

▸ How do we move on a grid? In what direction can we move?

▸ How is moving on a grid different from moving on a space without a grid?

For this activity, you will need the following materials:

- sidewalk chalk

- large outdoor space with a surface for chalk drawing

- yarn, yardstick, cardboard box (optional)

- playground ball(s)

Draw a large checkerboard-like grid outdoors using sidewalk chalk. Each square in the grid should be large enough for a child to stand inside it. Your school may already have a foursquare grid on the playground. You could expand or subdivide that grid with chalk.

If you would like to ensure an even grid with straight lines, use a long length of yarn and a yardstick. Hold or tape the yarn to the ground as a guide for drawing a straight line. Use a yardstick to measure the grid lines. Use any rectangular object, such as a book or a cardboard box, to check your right angles.

The children may enjoy helping you. Tell them you're making a grid for playing. Provide dotted lines to guide the path of the chalk.

Once the grid is finished, invite children to play in any way they please. As in the previous activity, they will likely adapt how they move to follow or align with the grid lines.

Use spatial reasoning vocabulary to describe what you see. Help the children identify when they are moving forward, backward, and sideways. You may introduce directionality, using the words "right" and "left," but be aware that most young children will not be able to identify right and left consistently until they are in first or second grade. The goal here is to help children understand that moving right or left means moving to one side or the other.

Add a bouncing ball to the outdoor play. Invite children to bounce a ball in their own square and then bounce it in another nearby square. Help the children identify where the ball has bounced—to the front, to the back, to one side, or to the other side.

Activity 3.3
Follow the Arrows

Arrows are important symbols. Understanding how to read and use arrows will benefit children as they learn to program robots. Arrows are frequently used in tangible tech devices and beginning coding apps and games.

As children explore the uses and meaning of arrows, they can ponder the following big questions:

▶ What is an arrow?

▶ How do people use arrows in our world?

For this activity, you will need large arrows drawn or printed onto pieces of paper, card stock, or index cards. Use one arrow per page or card, the bigger the better.

You could introduce the arrows to the children in an open way. For example, lay them out on a table or on the floor as a provocation that allows children to respond in any way they choose. Or you could introduce the arrow cards during group time by asking, "What do you think this symbol means?" Most children have probably seen arrows before and already understand that an arrow points in a direction to tell us which way to go. Invite the children to play with the arrows and place them around the school in ways that they think will be helpful to visitors and to one another. For example, ask, "How can we place the arrows in a way that will show people how to find the bathroom?" You could also encourage the children to use the arrows to play a form of hide-and-seek. One child hides, and another uses arrows (and no spoken words) to show a third child (or the teacher) how to find the hidden child.

Draw arrows on the playground using sidewalk chalk, as part of a checkerboard grid or free-form design. You might begin with a teacher-created example and invite children to follow the path. Then allow children to draw their own paths for you or their friends to follow.

Activity 3.4
Map Books

Reading and creating maps is a challenging task for young children. One fun, familiar way to introduce children to the concept of maps is through picture books. The following list provides some recommendations.

Map Books

- *As the Crow Flies: A First Book of Maps* by Gail Hartman

- *Follow That Map! A First Book of Mapping Skills* by Scot Ritchie

- *Henry's Map* by David Elliot

- *Mapping Penny's World* by Loreen Leedy

- *Me on the Map* by Joan Sweeney

- *My Map Book* by Sara Fanelli

- *There's a Map on My Lap! All about Maps* by Tish Rabe

**Books That Can Be Used to Talk about Maps
and Going from One Place to Another**

- *10 Little Rubber Ducks* by Eric Carle
- *Big Bug* by Henry Cole
- *Katy and the Big Snow* by Virginia Lee Burton
- *Lucy in the City* by Julie Dillemuth
- *Madlenka* by Peter Sís
- *Madlenka's Dog* by Peter Sís
- *Madlenka: Soccer Star* by Peter Sís
- *Rosie's Walk* by Pat Hutchins
- *Shrinking Mouse* by Pat Hutchins
- *Up, Down, and Around* by Katherine Ayres
- *Yellow Ball* by Molly Bang

All the books listed above lend themselves well to a follow-up activity that engages children in making their own maps on paper in ways that parallel the concepts in the books. One way to help children experiment with making a maplike drawing (if not an actual map) is providing graph paper instead of plain drawing paper and offering rubber stamps and ink pads for creating landmarks. These tools will help scaffold and support children as they learn to create a map. The tools allow children to simply draw lines and arrows between the landmarks. Don't worry if the children are not yet able to create a representation of an actual space or place. That will come over time, as their experience with maps, drawings, and spatial reasoning expands and develops.

Activity 3.5
Meet the Bee-Bots

This activity introduces children to a robotic device designed to teach coding concepts to children. I recommend Bee-Bot robots because they are very durable, and I have direct experience using them with children as young as three years old (www.bee-bot.us). There are other similar tools on the market, such as the Code & Go Robot Mouse (www.learningresources.com/product/learning+essentials--8482-+programmable+robot+mouse.do) and the Fisher-Price Code-a-pillar (www.fisher-price.com/en_US/brands/think-and-learn/products/Think-and-Learn-Code-a-pillar).

These robots are called tangible tech because they are stand-alone programmable devices. You don't need a computer or tablet to use them. Children don't need to interact with a screen or keyboard to tell the robots what to do. They tell the robot what to do by pushing buttons or, in the case of the Code-a-pillar, by attaching toy pieces together. Each push of a button or section of the chain is a command. The commands make up a sequence (also known as an algorithm, or a set of instructions), and that sequence becomes the code. In this way, children learn to program a robot.

The tangible tech robots are different from the mechanical toys suggested for use in chapter 2. Toys like Hexbugs or WowWee robotic animals are preprogrammed at the factory to perform specific actions. The children are not the programmers. Bee-Bots and the other tangible tech tools are interactive. They allow children to take the lead and code the robots to perform a sequence of commands.

As children play with tangible tech robots, they can ponder the following big questions:

▶ What can robots do?

▶ How do we tell robots what to do?

Bee-Bots and other educational coding devices often come with lesson plans, educator resources, scripts, and tools for direct instruction. I recommend that you first give children an opportunity to explore the devices without any instruction. This is inquiry-based learning at its best. Children will discover how the devices work through a constructivist, exploratory process, using trial and error.

Have the children use the robots in pairs. If you have more than one device, you could make space for two or three pairs of children to interact on the floor. Turn on the Bee-Bot using the on-off switch on the bottom of the device. Then hand the Bee-Bot to a child and see what happens. In most cases, children will figure out how to make the Bee-Bot go within a minute or two. They may not yet understand how to create a sequence of commands, but they will be satisfied immediately by their ability to make it move.

Each Bee-Bot has seven buttons on its back. The green GO button in the middle makes it go. But the Bee-Bot will not know how or where to go unless you first give it a command. Most children will quickly figure out through trial and error that

the four orange arrow buttons let the user command the robot to travel in a certain direction. To move forward one space, for example, you press once on the arrow pointing forward and then press GO.

There are also two blue buttons. The blue X button clears the code, and the blue button with parallel lines is a pause button. As children explore the device and try out different commands and sequences of commands, you may want to press the X button occasionally, when you know a child is ready to start a new sequence. Children who are just learning how to use the Bee-Bot will not yet understand that each time they add a command to the sequence and press GO, the Bee-Bot will continue to remember and perform all the commands previously included in the sequence. Pressing the X button when children are ready to start a new turn will help children make a cause-and-effect connection between the orange motion buttons and the movements of the Bee-Bot.

Most children will be engaged in playing with the Bee-Bots even before they understand how to create a sequence of commands intentionally. Allow children plenty of time to explore the Bee-Bots on multiple occasions before moving on to the other activities in this chapter, in which you will demonstrate specific coding strategies and concepts.

Once children consistently show understanding of how the buttons work, then it is time to move on to some of the next activities. You'll know the children are ready when their play with the Bee-Bot becomes more intentional. They will say things like "I can make the Bee-Bot go forward now." Alternatively, if children seem frustrated and no longer want to play with the Bee-Bot, that is an indicator that they need some guidance and are ready for next steps. In my own experience working with children and Bee-Bots, the children are rarely frustrated. Their questions and comments, such as "How do I make it follow me?" will lead to further activities, exploration, and learning.

Activity 3.6
Bee-Bot Hokey Pokey

Once they have had opportunities to play with a Bee-Bot in an open-ended way and have started to understand how a Bee-Bot works, most children will benefit from some teacher-guided learning about how to program these robots. In this activity, the teacher provides a playful demonstration that helps children become more intentional in planning and creating a sequence of commands.

As children do this activity, they can ponder the following big questions:

▸ Can a robot dance?

▸ How do we program a Bee-Bot to move "in" and "out," as in the hokey pokey?

This is a teacher-led and teacher-facilitated activity. Do it with the whole group of children at once. Hold up one of the Bee-Bots and ask the children, "Do you think we could program this Bee-Bot to do the hokey pokey?" Sing the song and invite the children to demonstrate the movements along with you. For the purposes of this demonstration, we won't move individual arms or legs, just the whole body.

As you stand in a circle and sing the song together, have the children act out the motions by moving their "whole self." Have the children jump in, then out, and then in again. Next, have everyone shake and turn around. For the last action, have the children clap their hands during the final words of the song.

Then ask the children for suggestions. How can we tell the Bee-Bot to move in, or move forward? If the children have had experience playing with a Bee-Bot, they will likely know that pushing the forward arrow button and then pressing GO will make the Bee-Bot move forward.

Then ask the children how to tell the Bee-Bot to move out, or move backward. Some will likely be able to suggest that you need to press the backward arrow button and then press GO. If a child makes another suggestion, one that is wrong or different, go ahead and try that one too. This will be an opportunity to demonstrate trial-and-error troubleshooting.

The children may think that to make the Bee-Bot go in and then out, they will need to follow a sequence like this:

1. Press forward.   3. Press backward.

2. Press GO.   4. Press GO.

You may need to explain to the children that the Bee-Bot can remember more than one command at a time. In fact, Bee-Bots can remember up to forty commands in a sequence. It's not necessary to press GO after each command.

Once you have successfully demonstrated how to program the Bee-Bot to go in and out, have the children dance and sing the first two lines of the song with the Bee-Bot.

If the children seem interested in programming the Bee-Bot to dance the whole song, you have an interesting challenge to consider. The Bee-Bot does not have a "shake it all about" button. Ask the children for ideas about how to solve this problem. They may suggest using the turn commands to make the Bee-Bot turn back and forth, right and left. If so, you'll discover that you need to slow down the pace of the singing during that part of the song as you wait for the Bee-Bot to finish shaking all about. The children might also suggest that the Bee-Bot rest during that part of the song while they do the shaking all about. This suggestion offers a great opportunity to demonstrate how the pause button works.

As a result, the full sequence of commands, or code, for a Bee-Bot hokey pokey may go something like this:

1. Press forward.   6. Press turn right.

2. Press backward.   7. Press turn right.

3. Press forward.   8. Press turn right.

4. Press pause.   9. Press turn right.

5. Press pause.   10. Press GO.

That's what coding's all about!

Activity 3.7
Turn Round and Round

The hokey pokey activity demonstrates to children an important use of the turn command. Not only can you use the turn command one time to make the Bee-Bot turn in a new direction, you can also use the turn command four times in a row to make the Bee-Bot turn all the way around in a circle.

As children continue to play with the Bee-Bot, they can ponder the following big questions:

▶ How does the Bee-Bot turn command work?

▶ What's the difference between the turn button on one side and the turn button on the other side?

The hokey pokey activity may inspire children to experiment with the turn commands without any teacher prompting. Some children, however, may need additional guidance and encouragement to experiment. You could say to the child, "I'm not sure I remember what we did before. Can you help me figure out how to tell the Bee-Bot to turn all the way around?" Or you could demonstrate turning your body all around and ask the child, "Can you make the Bee-Bot do what I just did?"

Encourage the children to count out loud and determine exactly how many times they need to push the turn button to make the Bee-Bot turn all the way around. The children may need your reminder or instructions to use the clear (X) button each time they start over with a new sequence of commands.

At some point, the children will likely discover that the Bee-Bot can turn all the way around in both directions. You could press the turn right button four times (and press GO), or you could press the turn left button four times (and press GO). This makes for a natural opportunity to introduce or remind the children that we have words for each direction; one is "right" and one is "left." Some children will be ready to explore this concept, and others will not. For now, all they really need to understand is that the buttons make Bee-Bot turn in opposite directions.

When children are in the process of deciding which direction they would like to make the Bee-Bot turn, ask them to demonstrate with their own bodies. They will either turn to the right (clockwise) or turn to the left (counterclockwise). Then ask the children to make the Bee-Bot match their own movements and travel in the same direction. Even if the children don't yet understand right, left, clockwise, or counterclockwise, they will probably still enjoy the challenge of making the Bee-Bot match their own movements.

Activity 3.8
Create a Path

As the children gain more experience programming the Bee-Bot, they will develop a clearer understanding of how to execute a sequence of commands. They will also become more intentional in how they use the Bee-Bot. Some of the children may be ready to program the Bee-Bot to follow a specific path—in other words, to travel from one point to another.

As children do this activity, they can ponder the following big questions:

▶ How do we program a Bee-Bot to get from one place to another?

▶ How do we troubleshoot or debug our code when we find that our program is not quite right?

To do this activity, you will need the following materials:

● Bee-Bot(s)

● painter's tape or sidewalk chalk

Create a brief, simple story in which the Bee-Bot is the main character. Perhaps the children have already done this during their play with and conversations about the Bee-Bots. For example, if one of the children pretends that the Bee-Bot is looking for a flower, make up a little story that goes "Once upon a time, a Bee-Bot needed pollen from a flower. It found a flower, and it was very happy. The end."

Then invite the children to program the Bee-Bot to act out the story. Use two props to represent the starting point and the ending point. A block could be the hive where the Bee-Bot lives, and a piece of colored paper could be the flower. Challenge the children to program the Bee-Bot to travel from the starting point to the ending point.

At first, make the path between the two points simple and direct, like a straight line. Once the children can successfully complete that challenge, reposition the starting and ending points to make the programming more difficult.

At some point, the child or children may struggle to complete the task successfully. This struggle offers a great opportunity to talk with children about troubleshooting or debugging. Tell the children that computer programmers and robotic engineers are continually making mistakes and improving their code. This is a natural part of the programming process.

If the children express frustration with not being able to see or remember their code, go to activity 3.10 (Invent a Programming Language). If the children seem to enjoy following short paths, try the next activity, 3.9 (Meet a Friend).

Activity 3.9
Meet a Friend

This activity is essentially the same as 3.8 (Create a Path). But in this activity, instead of using objects to show the starting and ending points, you use people. This creates a more social activity. The robot literally connects people. Using people instead of objects also makes a more exciting and unpredictable programming experience, because people often move around.

Be sure to show or remind the children that you can add commands to your sequence without starting over. For example, if you program the Bee-Bot to move forward four spaces, your code would include these commands:

1. Press forward.

2. Press forward.

3. Press forward.

4. Press forward.

5. Press GO.

But if you discover that after the Bee-Bot travels four spaces forward, you want it to turn right and move forward in that direction, you don't have to clear your code. You can simply add those two commands:

1. Press forward.	5. Turn right.
2. Press forward.	6. Press forward.
3. Press forward.	7. Press GO.
4. Press forward.	

Then, when you press GO, the Bee-Bot will perform all six commands in a sequence.

Activity 3.10
Invent a Programming Language

One benefit of a tangible tech device is that it is screenless. Children engage directly with the device; there is no need to view a screen on a smartphone, tablet, laptop, or desktop computer. The challenge, however, is that the device offers no visual representation of the commands the user has chosen and programmed by pushing the buttons on the back of the Bee-Bot. There is no visual record or history of the code. When you purchase a Bee-Bot from the manufacturer, some of the packages come with a set of cardboard command cards. You can line up these cards in a sequence on the floor or tabletop to create a visual record of the code. But I encourage you to hold off on introducing the cards to the children. Let them discover the need to keep a record of their code, to create a programming language that represents the Bee-Bot commands. Rest assured that the children will discover this need as a natural part of their play process. This independent discovery will have much more meaning and importance than an introduction by a teacher.

As children play with the Bee-Bots, they can ponder the following big questions:

▶ How do we remember what buttons we pushed on the Bee-Bot?

▶ How many ways can we show our code?

▶ What is a programming language?

For this activity, you will need the following materials:

- Bee-Bot(s)

- whatever materials children find or suggest to show their code (paper and crayons, colored blocks, arrow cards, pegs and pegboard, beads and string)

As the children gain more experience playing with the Bee-Bots, their play will become more and more intentional. The commands they choose and the buttons they push will become less random and more deliberate as they make decisions about where they want the Bee-Bot to travel. They may want the Bee-Bot to move between obstacles on the floor, or they may want the Bee-Bot to visit another Bee-Bot friend. The children will use trial and error to figure out how to program the Bee-Bot. Mistakes will occur, and the code will need changing or revising. This revising or troubleshooting process will require reflection. The children will need to remember what commands they used, but most children will not be able to remember more than a few commands at a time. They will discover the need to remember or record the commands. They may express this directly in words, such as "I can't remember what buttons I pushed!" Or they may simply become frustrated. Help children articulate what they need. For example, say, "You need a way to remember your code. You need a way to see your code so you know what buttons you pushed."

This is an exciting moment of discovery. The children will have discovered the need for a programming language. A programming language is any language people use to talk to computers or robots. At a more sophisticated level of computer science, there are languages such as Java and Python that have specific conventions, patterns, and syntax. At this introductory level of tangible tech, the Bee-Bot programming language, as represented by the buttons on the back of the device, is made up of symbols such as arrows and an X.

Ask the children, "What can we do to remember or show our code?" Some children may be able to articulate their ideas. Some may suggest that you write down arrows and Xs on a piece of paper. Some may remember the arrow cards you used in activity 3.3. Some children may have other novel and creative ideas. In my experience teaching with Bee-Bots, I've seen children represent their code with small plastic dinosaurs lined up in a row; each dinosaur was facing in the direction of the arrow or command. I've also seen children use markers laid out on the floor in a particular sequence of commands; the marker cap on each marker pointed in the direction of the command.

At some point in the process of creating a code to represent Bee-Bot commands, you may want to go ahead and introduce the Bee-Bot command cards from the manufacturer. The cards are well designed. Children can place them in a row to represent a long string of commands. But keep challenging children to think of their own ways to represent their code, such as placing colored blocks or puzzle pieces in a row, adding beads to a string, or lining up pegs on a pegboard. Each color could represent a direction or a command; for example, green means forward, red means back, blue means right, and orange means left.

Activity 3.11
Synchronize!

To synchronize means to coordinate the movements of two things, or to make them move together in the same way at the same time. Children may enjoy the challenge of synchronizing Bee-Bots, or programming multiple Bee-Bots to do exactly the same movements at the same time. This requires communication and collaboration among the children.

As children work together to synchronize Bee-Bots, they can ponder the following big questions:

▷ What does the word "synchronize" mean?

▷ How do we synchronize our Bee-Bots?

For this activity, you will need two or more Bee-Bots. Conduct the activity with a small group of children. The size of your group depends on how many Bee-Bots you have. I think three or four children make the ideal group size, but you could try this with as few as two or as many as six children in a group.

Explain to the children that you are going to learn to synchronize the Bee-Bots. Explain that to synchronize means to make things happen at the same time. You may want to demonstrate a sequence of synchronized movements using your own body, perhaps with another adult. For example, announce and move together to a simple sequence such as the following: step forward, step back, turn right, turn left.

Give each child or pair of children a Bee-Bot. Have the children line up on the floor in a row. Assign a command leader, a child who will decide and announce the sequence of commands. Invite that child to demonstrate the program that everyone will follow. The sequence should be fairly short so everyone will have a chance both to lead and follow. The leader will announce the code while programming a Bee-Bot, pausing after each command to give everyone a chance to do the same. For example, the leader might say, "Press forward," push the forward button on the Bee-Bot, and pause a moment while the other children push their forward buttons too. After five or six commands, it's time to test the synchronization. The leader can say, "Ready, set, go!" If everyone presses GO at the same time, the Bee-Bots should move in a fairly synchronized fashion. The children may need to troubleshoot the process to ensure that they've all coded their Bee-Bots with the exact same commands and that everyone presses GO at the same time. Repeat this activity until everyone has had a chance to be the leader.

This synchronization activity provides an opportunity for children to observe how the Bee-Bots are calibrated. The word "calibrated" means that the distance a Bee-Bot travels each time it executes a forward or backward command is always roughly the same (about six inches). The children may spontaneously note the fact that the Bee-Bots all travel at the same speed and cover the same distance. If the topic comes up, you may choose to introduce activity 3.13 (DIY Grid), in which the children measure and mark the space the Bee-Bot travels.

Activity 3.12
Bee-Bot Dance

In this activity, we take synchronization one step further. In addition to synchronizing the Bee-Bots, the children synchronize their own bodies to match the movements of the Bee-Bots. As they do so, they can ponder the following big questions:

▸ Can we move our bodies like a Bee-Bot?

▸ How do we make Bee-Bots dance?

For this activity, I recommend you use only two Bee-Bots so you'll have enough floor space for the children to move around. Depending on the size of your classroom, you may also want to limit each group to three or four children.

Have the children synchronize the movements of two Bee-Bots in the same manner as activity 3.11. After they have tested and debugged the sequence of commands and are satisfied that the Bee-Bots are ready, have the children stand up and move their bodies to match the movements of the Bee-Bots. They may need you to demonstrate or point out to them that when the Bee-Bot moves backward, its face still points forward. Sometimes when children are imitating the Bee-Bots, the direction of their movement is synchronized correctly, but their orientation—the way they are facing—is not. This activity may be surprisingly difficult for children, as it involves both kinesthetic and spatial reasoning. But children will probably still have fun trying it.

Add music! When we call the Bee-Bot movements a "dance" and perform the actions along with music, the rhythm and choreography of the Bee-Bot actions becomes more lively and interesting. Music may inspire children to come up with new combinations of commands to coordinate with specific songs.

Activity 3.13
DIY Grid

Synchronization activities call attention to the fact that Bee-Bots all move at pretty much the same pace and cover the same distance. The manufacturer calibrates the devices to do so. The space a Bee-Bot travels each time it moves forward or backward is about six inches.

You can purchase a grid (a large mat marked with six-inch squares) from the Bee-Bot supplier. If you are following an inquiry approach that allows children to investigate, explore, and discover through play, you may want to wait to introduce the grid until after children notice and take interest in the distance the Bee-Bot travels. In fact, the children may enjoy making their own grid or map.

As children play with Bee-Bots and observe their movements, they can ponder the following big questions:

▸ How far does a Bee-Bot travel each time it moves?

▸ How can we measure or draw the distance a Bee-Bot travels?

▸ How do we make a map or grid that shows how a Bee-Bot moves?

To do this activity, you will need the following materials:

● Bee-Bot(s)

● large paper and markers, or painter's tape

● ruler or a nonstandard measuring tool, such as a unit block

With a small group of children, demonstrate how a Bee-Bot moves forward one space or one command. Ask the children, "How far does the Bee-Bot go?" If the children have had any previous experience with measurement, they may have some ideas or suggestions. If not, ask them, "How can we show or measure how far a Bee-Bot goes each time it moves forward?" You could put the Bee-Bot on a piece of paper and mark with a crayon or pencil the spot where the front of the Bee-Bot is positioned before it moves, and then mark the spot where it is positioned after it moves one space forward. You could measure that distance with a ruler, or you could ask the children to find an object in the room that matches that length.

A standard unit block, for example, is five and one-half inches long—almost the same distance a Bee-Bot will travel.

Use painter's tape on the floor, or use a big piece of paper and a marker, to create a line or path for the Bee-Bot to follow. Mark with tape or a line at each interval where the Bee-Bot stops or pauses. The children probably will not be able to do this independently. They will need a teacher to lead and facilitate this process, but they can be active participants.

After you've marked the intervals on the line, add perpendicular lines at the intervals. Then add some additional grid lines until you have a Bee-Bot–size grid. Invite children to play with the Bee-Bots on the grid in an open-ended way. The grid lines will provide a visible structure for the Bee-Bot movements and allow children to become even more intentional about programming the Bee-Bots.

Once you've made a grid for the Bee-Bots, help the children make connections between the Bee-Bot grid and the checkerboard play from activities 3.1 and 3.2. Revisit the big grid from activity 3.2 outdoors, this time using the arrow cards from activity 3.3 to represent the children's movements as they move their own bodies from one square to another. They may enjoy programming one another or programming their teacher in the same way they have created commands for the Bee-Bots. For example, one child could take the arrow cards and lay them down in a sequence of commands: move forward, move right, move forward, move right. The other child or adult, who is playing the role of the Bee-Bot, stands on the grid and jumps or steps from one square to another, following the code: move forward, move right, move forward, move right.

Activity 3.14
Meet Cubetto

Bee-Bots are not the only educational robotic device available for schools to purchase. While you're reading this book, more are being invented and marketed. You can do the activities in the first part of this chapter (activities 3.1 through 3.13) with any device that you can program to navigate a grid.

Another device you could use is the Code & Go Robot Mouse (www.learning resources.com/product/learning+essentials--8482-+programmable+robot

+mouse.do). The Robot Mouse is a bit smaller and less expensive than the Bee-Bot. Unlike the Bee-Bot, the Robot Mouse does not use a rechargeable battery. The Robot Mouse needs three AAA batteries, which you must replace when they wear out. I have often used this tool with children, but the Robot Mouse has one feature I do not like: the red button is a random command. When you use this command in your code, you can't predict what action it will do. I feel this feature undermines children's understanding of logic—the ability to plan and predict as they create code—that children develop as they play with these devices. When I use the Robot Mouse with children, I usually tape over the red button so they can't use it.

A number of wonderful robotic devices are appropriate for young children but require the use of a tablet or smartphone. One example is Dash and Dot from Wonder Workshop (www.makewonder.com). Another example is the popular Sphero BB-8 robot (www.sphero.com). These devices can be used in classrooms, but they require the additional hardware of a tablet or smartphone to program and operate the devices.

I recommend the Bee-Bot robots to teachers and schools because they require no additional hardware. They are true tangible tech because they are screenless. Many would argue that children are already spending too much time looking at screens at school and at home. Any opportunity to teach computational thinking, logic, and robotics engineering concepts away from screens is a welcome alternative. And, as described in activity 3.10, the absence of a screen challenges the children to come up with their own creative ways to represent their code, a twenty-first-century example of Loris Malaguzzi's "hundred languages of children."

There is one other tangible tech device, in addition to the Bee-Bot, that I frequently recommend. It is the Cubetto (www.primotoys.com). Cubetto is a small robot on wheels, similar to the Bee-Bot. The design is simple and appealing. In fact, this product meets Montessori standards as a beautiful and functional classroom tool. Unlike the Bee-Bot, the Cubetto does not have buttons on its back. The robot comes with a board. Each command, such as "move forward" or "turn right," is represented by a colorful block. Children place the command blocks on the board in a sequence. There is a wireless connection between the board and the robot. When the child presses the GO button on the board, the Cubetto robot performs the sequence of commands.

Like the Bee-Bot, Cubetto is sold with a number of different grid mats, called maps. The maps are beautifully designed as well. They represent different kinds of

settings, such as outer space or underwater. However, I recommend that teachers provide frequent opportunities for children to play with the Cubetto in an open-ended manner before introducing the maps or a homemade grid. This allows children to discover on their own what the robot can do, as well as imagine their own stories or scenarios.

I also recommend the Cubetto "Teacher's Guide," which is a free downloadable resource found here: www.primotoys.com/wp-content/uploads/2016/04 /Cubetto_teachers_guide.pdf. The teacher's guide describes how to introduce the Cubetto robot to young children as a "friendly robot" that will follow their instructions and do what they tell it to do. You can demonstrate how the blocks work or allow the children to experiment and learn through trial and error. Most young children will be able to figure out how to make the Cubetto move in a short time. The "Teacher's Guide" suggests that you start with a three-block sequence, until the children become more familiar with the programming process.

Activity 3.15
The Cubetto Function Line

The Cubetto robot has one exceptional feature that most other robotic devices currently on the market don't offer. The Cubetto board has a function line. In computer science, the word "function" is a special coding term. A function is a shortcut, a way of abbreviating your code to make it more efficient. Sometimes programmers use the word "elegant" to describe code that is written with great efficiency and simplicity.

The Cubetto function line allows the user to place up to four command blocks inside a special area on the pegboard designated as the function line, and then use a single block, the blue function block, to represent all the commands in the function line. For example, suppose you want the Cubetto robot to move forward four times. You would place four green forward blocks on the function line, then place the one blue function block at the beginning of the programming queue. When you press GO and activate your program, the Cubetto robot moves forward four times.

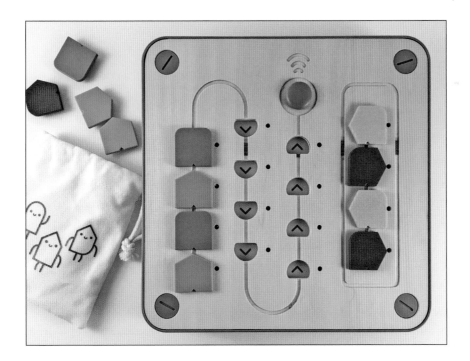

Now suppose you want the robot to move forward four times, turn left, then move forward four times, turn right, and then move forward again four times. Because you already have four forward blocks on your function line, all you would need to include in your queue are the following blocks:

1. Function block

2. Turn left block

3. Function block

4. Turn right block

5. Function block

You have abbreviated your code, which consists of fourteen commands, and represented it with only five blocks in your queue. This concept of using a function line to create elegant code may seem sophisticated to a nonprogrammer, but the Cubetto robot allows young children to gain hands-on experience with this coding challenge through a developmentally appropriate play experience.

Activity 3.16
Code-a-pillar

In summer 2016, the Fisher-Price toy company introduced a coding device called Code-a-pillar (www.fisher-price.com/en_US/brands/think-and-learn/products /Think-and-Learn-Code-a-pillar). The Code-a-pillar is recommended for children ages three to six. This device is truly a tangible tech experience because it requires no additional hardware, such as a tablet, laptop, or smartphone. Children take an active role in programming the toy to move and make sounds. Each segment of the caterpillar-like robot represents a different command, such as "move forward" or "turn right." Little hands can easily snap the pieces together to create a sequence from the front to the back. When the child presses the GO button near the head of the Code-a-pillar, the robot will perform the commands in order.

When I tested this device for use in early childhood classrooms, the issue I encountered is that the robot is very loud. Every time you press GO, the device plays music and makes loud beeps and other robotic sounds. This could be a real distraction in a busy early childhood classroom. It could also be overwhelming for children who are sensitive to sensory stimulation.

I wrote to Fisher-Price and asked if there is a way to mute or eliminate the sounds. The company responded to say that was not possible in the current design. However, recently I found a way to hack the Code-a-pillar and disable the sound. I removed the batteries and opened up the main section of the device by unscrewing the four silver screws with a Phillips screwdriver. I couldn't fully remove the cover from the base, because wires connect the main device to the lights and the speaker on the underside of the cover. But I was able to identify the blue wire that connects the speaker to the main device, and I simply snipped that wire. Now my Code-a-pillar is completely silent, but all the other functions still work perfectly.

I predict that Fisher-Price will continue to improve this product and eventually offer versions that allow users to adjust the volume or mute the sounds. I do think this device has a lot of potential for teaching children how to code a robot—to create a sequence of commands that tell a robot what to do. Many of the other activities included in this book could be done successfully using a Code-a-pillar.

Activity 3.17
Robot Turtle Board Game

Here's an idea for another screen-free experience that engages children in coding. Robot Turtles is a board game with cards and playing pieces made of good old-fashioned cardboard. No electronic devices are required to play this game, although an e-book is sold separately by the game company. Children as young as four years can play the game at an introductory level, with an adult facilitator.

The game board looks a bit like a checkerboard, with grid lines. Each player has a cardboard turtle as a playing piece. The object of the game is to program your turtle to get to a jewel. Command cards represent your program. One playing card represents each command, such as "move forward" or "turn right." Players select their cards one at a time to "code" the movements of their turtles.

The game instructions suggest that the adult be the one to actually move the turtle across the board, because that's similar to how a real computer works. The programmer tells the computer what to do. However, my experience playing this game shows that children really like to move their own game pieces. No matter who moves the pieces, children will still learn about how to create a sequence of code, or an algorithm, that directs the path of the turtle.

What I love most about this game is the Bug card that can be played at any time to fix or "de-Bug" your code. This feature makes debugging and mistakes a normal part of the process, just like STEM learning in real life.

For children who are older or ready for additional challenges, you can introduce walls by adding obstacle cards to the board. The website www.robotturtles.com also provides sample mazes and user-generated mazes that you can use to add a greater challenge.

Activity 3.18
People Patterns

This activity and the next four are "unplugged" activities. They are activities that introduce young children to many of the same STEM concepts and ideas they can learn through robotic devices like Bee-Bots and Cubetto, yet without the need to purchase new equipment. You can do these activities with materials and people found in any early childhood classroom.

For this activity, you will need three or four small dolls or people figures. You will show the children how they can position the toys in a line to show what you want your friend, or your teacher, to do.

As children make people patterns, they can ponder the following big questions:

▸ How can we use toys to show other people what we want them to do?

▸ How might we position a toy to show a motion?

▸ Does the order of the toys matter? Why or why not?

Show a small group of children the dolls and explain that you are going to teach them a new way to play with the dolls. Tell the children, "You can place the dolls in a row to show people how to move." Place three dolls in a row—one facing forward, one facing to the right, and one facing to the left. Have the children stand up and follow along as you demonstrate the movements represented by the sequence of dolls. Stand facing forward, turn to one side, then turn to the other side. The children don't need to know the words "right" and "left," only that they turn one way first and turn the other way next.

Invite one of the children to move the three dolls another way, and have the group act out that sequence of actions too. Point to each doll as you perform each action so that the children get a sense of the sequence from left to right, one action at a time.

The children may come up with their own ideas for actions that the dolls or people figures can represent. If the dolls bend, the children could create a sequence that includes sitting down and then standing up. If the legs on the dolls don't bend, the sequence could include lying down.

You could introduce other toys to symbolize other movements. A toy rabbit could represent a hop, for example. Or, instead of motions, the toys could represent animal sounds. For example, a cow could symbolize mooing, a pig could symbolize oinking, and so on.

The important thing is that the children learn to read the code from left to right. Then they perform each action in the order represented by the order of the toys.

Activity 3.19
Pattern Blocks

Most early childhood classrooms are equipped with colored building blocks or parquetry tiles that are used for open-ended construction and patterning play. You can use these materials to teach children how to create a sequence of commands (a code). But instead of programming a robot, the children will program each other. As they do so, children can ponder the following big questions:

▶ How can we use shapes and colors to show how we move?

▶ How can we create a code with blocks or tiles?

In a small group, create a simple sequence of three colored blocks, shapes, or parquetry tiles. Set the sequence in a row on a tabletop or on the floor. For example, you might arrange the following:

1. Triangle

2. Circle

3. Triangle

Explain to the children that each shape represents an action, something we can do. For example, you could say that the triangle means clap your hands. The circle means blow a kiss. Demonstrate the sequence to the children as you point to each shape:

1. Point to the triangle and clap your hands.

2. Point to the circle and blow a kiss.

3. Point to the triangle and clap your hands.

Invite the children to do the actions along with you. Then ask one of the children to change the order of the three blocks. Perhaps now the order is this:

1. Triangle

2. Triangle

3. Circle

Invite the children to read the sequence and do the actions with you, like this:

1. Point to the triangle and clap your hands.

2. Point to the triangle and clap your hands.

3. Point to the circle and blow a kiss.

Invite the children to add more circles or more triangles to the sequence. Then challenge the children to act out the new, longer sequence.

Once the children have learned how to create a sequence of commands and act them out using the two variables you suggested, see if they can come up with their own ideas. Perhaps a square will mean touch your nose, or a diamond will mean stamp your feet.

Some children may also show an interest in using the color of the block to carry some meaning in the code. If a block is red, that could mean you must do the action quickly. If it's blue, that could mean do it slowly.

As children learn to play with these variables and variations, they are creating more complex algorithms. An algorithm is a set of instructions for completing a task or solving a problem. This is what computer programmers do when they create code for robots to execute specific actions and functions. A sequence of code is an algorithm.

Activity 3.20
Arrow Maps

Earlier in this chapter, children learned to use the universal symbol of the arrow to show the direction of travel. They posted large arrows on a wall or laid them on the floor. The placement of the arrows in the environment provided context clues that helped the children understand how to interpret the arrows.

In this activity, children learn to create a sequence of arrows on a piece of paper that they carry in their hands. As they do so, they can ponder the following big questions:

▶ What is an arrow?

▶ How do people use arrows?

For this activity, you will need an arrow template and markers, crayons, or pencils. An arrow template is a linear grid with just eight spaces, such as this:

Use this template to draw a few short and simple arrow sequences. For example, the first time children use this grid, fill in only two or three squares with arrows. Start on the top left and move from left to right, top to bottom. A simple introductory sequence might be left arrow, right arrow, left arrow.

Hand the page to a child. Stand behind the child to offer guidance as the child figures out how to follow the arrows. Point to the left arrow in the first space and say, "Turn this way." Show the child how to turn in the direction of the arrow. Then point to the right arrow in the second space and say, "Turn this way." Show the child how to turn in the direction of the second arrow. Then point to the left arrow in the third space and say, "Turn this way." Show the child how to turn in the direction of the arrow.

Learning to read and follow the arrow instructions may be challenging for some children. They may be more interested in creating arrow instructions for you and watching you follow them. This interaction will be similar to what happens when a child begins learning to write letters and hands a page of randomly ordered but carefully written letters to an adult and asks, "What did I write?" In this case, however, the adult can probably make some sense of the child's instructions. Meanwhile, the child gets the satisfaction of having the power to tell an adult what to do.

Some children may have difficulty drawing their own arrows. If that occurs, you can purchase arrow rubber stamps or arrow stickers from many office supply stores.

Activity 3.21
Program Your Parents

You can share with families any of the three previous activities (3.18 through 3.20). Families can do these "coding" activities together at home. Take photos of children's people codes or block codes. Make some blank copies of arrow templates. Send these home to families, or plan for an unplugged coding activity for your next family meeting or event.

Activity 3.22
Rebus Stories

This activity reinforces the concept of a symbol—a drawing or figure that represents something else. This activity also reinforces the idea that people use symbols in a sequence to create meaning. The meaning can be code for a robot or, in this case, the meaning can be a story.

As you read a rebus story with the children, they can ponder the following big question:

▶ What stories can we tell with pictures?

For this activity, you will need the following materials:

- variety of rubber stamps

- ink pads with washable ink

- paper

- pencils, crayons, or markers

In a rebus story, a picture represents words or letters. Reading rebus stories in books and creating our own rebus stories on paper helps reinforce the concept of symbols. It also teaches children that something small can represent something bigger, just like the code we create in computer programming.

Read a rebus story out loud to a small group of children, pointing to each of the small pictures as you read the text. Each issue of *Highlights* magazine usually features a rebus. Your local library may also carry rebus books, such as *The Rebus Treasury* by Jean Marzollo or the Rebus Read-Along Story series by Alyssa Satin Capucilli.

Invite the children to create and dictate their own rebus stories using rubber stamps for the pictures. First, the children may enjoy just experimenting with the rubber stamps and making their own pictures and patterns on paper. As they work, ask, "Who has some words to add to their story?" Offer to write the words on the page, next to the stamped pictures children have already created, or write the words first and then have the children add a stamped picture to each sentence.

Don't worry if the inked pictures do not align correctly with the text you write. The important idea here is that children have an experience using small pictures or icons as symbols.

Coding Apps and Websites

The last five activities in this chapter describe digital tools, such as applications (apps) or websites, that teach children how to code. If you have tablets or laptops available for your classroom, you may want to consider these digital coding tools. You don't need to have a device for every child in your class. In fact, research shows that children learn more when they work in pairs on tablets than when they use tablets alone (Blackwell 2015).

Any use of digital tools in an early childhood classroom must be carefully considered. A good place to start is the joint position statement created by NAEYC and the Fred Rogers Center (FRC) for Early Learning and Children's Media at Saint Vincent College. This statement is titled *Technology and Interactive Media as Tools in Early Childhood Programs Serving Children from Birth through Age 8*. For guidance on whether to use coding apps with young children, we can look to this section of the statement:

> Developmentally appropriate teaching practices must always guide the selection of any classroom materials, including technology and interactive media.
>
> Teachers must take the time to evaluate and select technology and media for the classroom, carefully observe children's use of the materials to identify opportunities and problems, and then make appropriate adaptations. They must be willing to learn about and become familiar with new technologies as they are introduced and be intentional in the choices they make, including ensuring that content is developmentally appropriate and that it communicates anti-bias messages. (NAEYC and FRC 2012, 6)

The three primary apps that I describe and recommend here (Daisy the Dinosaur, Kodable, and ScratchJr) meet NAEYC guidelines in that they have been reviewed and evaluated by respected educators and advocacy groups such as Common Sense Media. In the Leapfrog program I coordinate at Northwestern University, we have used these apps in classrooms over the past two years. I've worked with about fifty different instructors, and our coding courses have served almost one thousand children. We've observed the children's use of these tools, and we even invited a research team to study how our youngest students use the apps. I feel confident recommending them to other educators, with one caveat: In our Leapfrog classrooms, we limit the amount of time children use tech devices to ensure that children's classroom experience, even in the coding classes, is well balanced with other kinds of play and learning. We use the coding activities in one small learning center that the children visit in small groups.

A reliable and respected source of app and game reviews is the non-profit organization Common Sense. You can find it on the web at www.commonsensemedia.org.

> Common Sense is the leading independent nonprofit organization dedicated to helping kids thrive in a world of media and technology. We empower parents, teachers, and policymakers by providing unbiased information, trusted advice, and innovative tools to help them harness the power of media and technology as a positive force in all kids' lives. (Common Sense, accessed 2017)

Activity 3.23
Daisy the Dinosaur

Daisy the Dinosaur is a free educational app available for iPads. (Visit www.daisythedinosaur.com.) Currently it is not available for Android tablets.

The app teaches children to create a sequence of commands that will program the animated character of Daisy the Dinosaur to perform various actions. The app uses block programming, which means that each command appears on the screen as a labeled color block. Children use the touch screen to move the blocks or commands from the left side, where the menu of commands appears, to the desktop or workspace on the top right side of the screen. The code becomes stacked vertically from top to bottom. When you press play, Daisy performs the commanded actions.

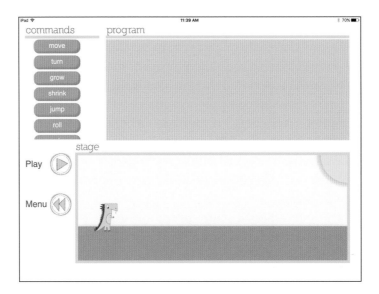

Daisy the Dinosaur is a great app for beginning coders because the animation is simple, with few distractions. Daisy is the only character, and the background never changes. The yellow sun always shines in Daisy's world.

The problem with using Daisy the Dinosaur with young children is that the blocks are labeled with text instead of with symbols or icons. Prereaders will have a harder time using this app, at least initially, than children who can read. The good news is that, in my experience, children learn how to use the app more by trial and error than by reading. They quickly figure out that the first block at the top of the commands menu is the move command even if they are not able to read the word "move." In fact, the children are so highly motivated to learn how to animate Daisy with code that many develop the ability to read the words as sight vocabulary even before they have learned the names of the letters or how to decode text.

In classrooms where we have used Daisy the Dinosaur with prereaders, we have created a poster that gives the children a key for understanding the commands.

The Daisy the Dinosaur app also introduces children to two important coding concepts: looping and conditions. The *repeat* command is an example of looping. The *when* command is an example of conditions.

Activity 3.24
Kodable

Kodable is an educational game that teaches coding. The player must create a sequence of commands to guide a little, fuzzy creature through a maze to capture coins. This app is available for both iPads and Android tablets. (Visit www.kodable .com.)

The app is free for the introductory level of play. But if you want the option to progress to more complex levels, you will find pricing options for schools and school districts. You can also try out Kodable online in a web-based tutorial here: https://game.kodable.com/hour-of-code.

I recommend the introductory level of Kodable as a great introduction to coding for young children. No reading is required to play the game. The children use a finger on the touch screen to move the commands, each indicated by an arrow that points up, down, left, or right. The menu of arrow commands appears on the top right, and the player moves each command to the workspace on the top left.

The game has a built-in tutorial that helps players learn what to do. For example, if the player needs to select the up arrow next, that arrow begins to glow and pulse, directing the player's attention to that command.

Young children seem to enjoy the fuzzy characters in the game. In our Leapfrog classrooms where we use Kodable, the children make their own Kodable creatures to take home by gluing googly eyes onto yarn pom-poms.

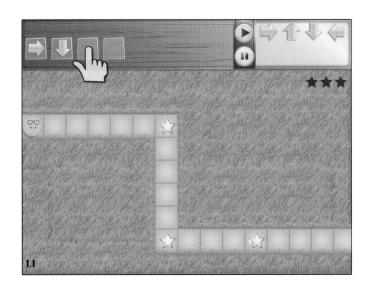

Activity 3.25
ScratchJr

ScratchJr is a free educational app available for both iPads and Android tablets. (Visit www.scratchjr.org.) But ScratchJr is more than just a game or a lesson in coding. ScratchJr is a programming language that allows children to create animated stories and games. The ScratchJr programming language is made up of individual blocks that children move on the touch screen with a finger. The programming blocks snap together in a sequence to make the characters move, speak, sing, and make sound effects.

ScratchJr offers a big menu of different characters to animate and backgrounds to choose. It also includes tools for children to draw their own characters and backgrounds or to take photos of themselves or their friends and family to incorporate into their stories.

ScratchJr was inspired by the popular Scratch programming language for older children (https://scratch.mit.edu). One of the lead creators of ScratchJr was Marina Umaschi Bers, mentioned in the introduction of this book as one of the leading minds in developmentally appropriate robotics and tangible tech. She is a co-author, with Mitchel Resnick, of *The Official ScratchJr Book: Help Your Kids Learn to Code*, an excellent resource for how to get started teaching ScratchJr.

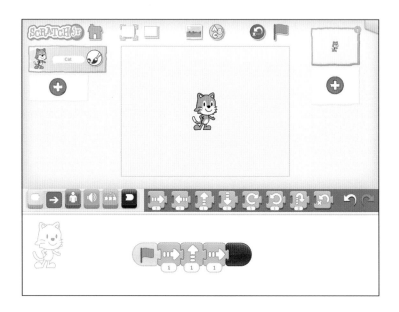

Activity 3.26
Other Coding Apps

You can try a number of other well-reviewed educational apps that teach coding to children. These include Lightbot and The Foos.

Lightbot is a game in which the player chooses commands represented by arrows to program an animated robot to travel on a small grid to reach a light-bulb. When each challenge is successfully completed, the lightbulb will glow. The introductory "Hour of Code" version of Lightbot is free but the full app requires a purchase. For more information about Lightbot, visit https://lightbot.com.

The Foos is a game in which players (ages four years and older) earn points by programming the animated characters to accomplish different tasks. This app is available for purchase for both iPads and Android tablets. For more information about The Foos, visit http://thefoos.com. A CodeSpark curriculum has been developed for The Foos and is available to download at http://thefoos.com/coding -resources-for-you.

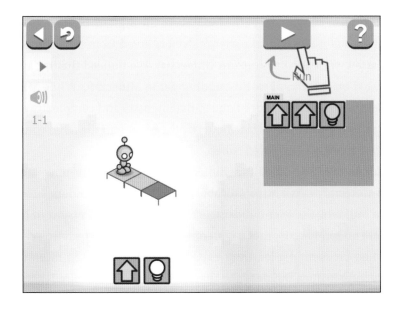

Activity 3.27
Build Your Code

Parents and educators often express concern about screen time. A growing body of evidence indicates that children of all ages are spending more and more time engaging with screens at home and at school (Joan Ganz Cooney Center, accessed 2017).

This doesn't necessarily mean that we should eliminate screens. However, we do need to make sure that the digital tools we use are safe and effective learning tools, and that they are developmentally appropriate for young children.

I believe that one way we can make the most of children's digital learning experiences is to look for every opportunity to help children make meaningful connections between the virtual, digital world and the real, tangible world. We already know, through the work of the Reggio Emilia schools and the followers of Lilian Katz's project approach, that when children are challenged to represent what they know using more than one medium, their learning becomes much deeper and more meaningful. The same must be true when children move from the digital to the tangible and back again from the tangible to the digital.

I can share one successful experience I've observed from the Leapfrog coding classes where I work at Northwestern University. We noticed that many children are fascinated by the digital world-building game Minecraft. While Minecraft is not appropriate for young children due to the intensity and complexity of some of the features, every child seems fascinated by the Minecraft idea that you can build whatever you need out of colored cubes.

A world-building app called Toca Builders is, in some ways, a kinder and gentler version of Minecraft. (Visit https://tocaboca.com/app/toca-builders.)

In Toca Builders, the user builds structures out of cubes, just as in Minecraft. But there are no zombies or other frightening features. In our Leapfrog classrooms, we've created cross-media learning experiences that allow children to build a virtual structure in Toca Builders and then build that same or similar structure in the real world using foam cube blocks. We've also done this activity the other way around. A child can build a tangible structure with blocks in the real world and then use the Toca Builders app to make a virtual replica of the structure.

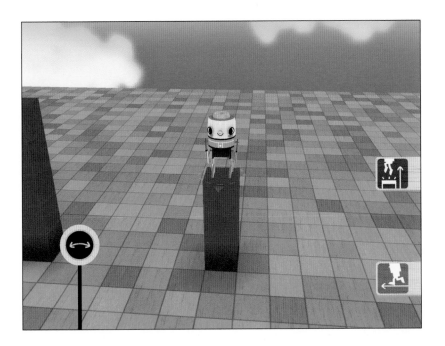

I believe that cross-media learning experiences like these will become even more essential for deep learning as classrooms and curricula become more digital and virtual. Children will always need to learn with their hands as well as with their brains.

4

How Do Robots Help Us?

Imagining a Better World

Learning about robots is a valuable experience relevant to all aspects of STEM education. Most children enjoy learning how robots work, how they're made, and how to program them. But does the value of robotics extend beyond the classroom? Some might argue that robots are only a trend or fad. Do we really need robots in our lives, or are we perhaps just caught up in a consumer-driven society that continually develops fancier electronic devices so tech companies can make more money?

When I hear people say that we would all be better off without advanced technology like computers and robots, I think about what happens when someone is injured or ill and gets rushed to a hospital emergency room. Computerized or robotic tools like digital thermometers, MRI machines, and laser scalpels are essential to saving lives and helping people heal and stay well. Advancements in health care alone are a cogent argument for the benefits of technology and, specifically, robotics. Improved efficiency and safety in industry and transportation are other examples of ways computers and robots help make the world a better place.

The activities in this chapter help children imagine how robots can play a positive role in their own lives, in the lives of the people they love, and in the lives of people all over the world. "A high-quality computing education equips pupils to use computational thinking and creativity to understand and change the world" (UK Department for Education 2013). Let's help children create a world where robots are heroes, not villains; where children use their hands and brains to innovate and invent; and where everyone has a role in creating solutions and advancements that improve all our lives.

The ideas in this chapter extend children's growing understanding of robotics. These activities and resources will help children apply their ideas and skills to new situations and contexts. Rather than following a prescribed sequence, these activities are intended to provide a path based on children's emergent interests. Read through this chapter, and then be a vigilant observer and listener for cues in children's play and conversations that indicate they are ready to pursue one of these topics.

Activity 4.1
Robot Helpers

To develop or extend a conversation about how robots might help people, read aloud the picture book *Robot Rumpus* by Sean Taylor. In this fanciful story, a family enlists the help of a team of silly robots to accomplish a variety of household chores. The robots include Cook-bot, Wash-bot, Dry-bot, and Clean-bot. When the sensors on Wash-bot malfunction, chaos ensues. The book is funny, colorful, and engaging, though not an accurate representation of how robots really work.

Afterward ask the children, "Could this story really happen? Why or why not?" Listen to their responses without correcting any misconceptions. Engaging in a conversation that challenges children to articulate why they believe something helps develop critical thinking.

Then show children the photos in the nonfiction picture book *Robots at Home* by Christine Zuchora-Walske. The robots in this book are real-life examples of useful robots that serve families.

Here's another nonfiction resource about helpful robots: "The Year in Robots" by Bob Tedeschi (http://www.nytimes.com/2014/12/25/garden/10-home-robots -to-lighten-your-domestic-chores.html). This *New York Times* photo-essay shows examples of robots that can do the following jobs:

- water your lawn

- scrub your floors

- rock your baby

- clean your grill

- mow your lawn

- clean your cat's litter box

Once children have had a chance to learn more about real robots that can help people clean and do chores, revisit the book *Robot Rumpus*. Talk again about what could really happen and what is pretend. Some of the children's ideas and opinions may have changed or evolved in interesting ways.

Activity 4.2
Robot Pets

Can a robot provide comfort and companionship? This is a question to explore through reading stories, viewing video clips, discussion, and play.

Andrea Baruffi's picture book *If I Had a Robot Dog* provides a great introduction to the topic of robot pets. After reading it with the children, ask them to think about the similarities and differences between a robot dog and a real dog. Write children's ideas on a two-column chart or Venn diagram.

If possible, compare an actual robot to an actual dog, or a toy robot dog to a stuffed animal toy dog. Here are some examples:

- Tekno robotic puppy (www.tekno-robotics.com/robotic-puppy5g)

- Paw Patrol toys (https://shop.spinmaster.com/store/us/paw-patrol/_/N-q3emjg)

- FurReal Friends (www.hasbro.com/en-us/brands/furreal)

I don't recommend purchasing these toys for ongoing classroom use. Most are not durable enough to last long in a busy early childhood classroom. But if you can borrow one for demonstration purposes, that would be ideal.

Some robotic toy dogs have fur, and some do not. That sensory difference will likely be a significant point of discussion for the children.

Some engineers have developed robots that provide comfort, companionship, and other pet-like services to humans. One example is the SpotMini robot dog

(http://thekidshouldseethis.com/post/boston-dynamics-new-spotmini-robot).
Another example is PARO, a therapeutic robot that looks like a baby seal. (See www
.parorobots.com and www.nytimes.com/video/us/1247468152153/bonding-with
-paro.html.)

If you plan to use the PARO video mentioned above, remember this important
note about using Internet videos in an early childhood classroom. Most young
children are visual learners. Educational videos can bring exciting new ideas and
inspiration into your classroom. Early childhood educators have a responsibility to
carefully consider the role of media in the lives of young children. Use the princi-
ples outlined in the NAEYC position paper on the use of technology and interactive
media as a guide for making these decisions (www.naeyc.org/files/naeyc/file
/positions/PS_technology_WEB2.pdf).

In my experience, viewing a short video (three to five minutes long) can be an
engaging and informative tool for helping children understand STEM topics. I
think of these videos as a supplement to the children's core learning experience,
not the centerpiece of the activity. I recommend using a short video to introduce a
new topic, to begin a new conversation, to demonstrate an example of a new idea,
or to inspire a creative project.

The videos suggested in this book provide examples and information that
can't be found in other media, such as picture books. Always screen videos before
showing them to children. When you're preparing to use an Internet video in your
classroom, be sure to prepare the screen and browser window so that ads, pop-
ups, and other potentially inappropriate content are not visible to children. For
example, when you're viewing YouTube videos, the thumbnails of promoted videos
that appear on the right side of the screen are often inappropriate for children, even
when the primary video is clearly intended for a young audience. Open the video
in full-screen mode before showing it to children, or download the video to your
desktop. You may also want to consider ad-blocking software for your school or for
the personal device you use when you're teaching.

Activity 4.3
Robot Doctors

As you guide children in exploring ways robots can help make the world better and safer, one topic that might come up is the use of robots in health care. Robotic surgical devices are gaining sophistication and effectiveness, but the topic of surgery can be frightening to children and difficult to understand. I don't recommend initiating a discussion on the topic of robotic surgery, but if children bring it up, perhaps because they've seen something about it on TV or because a family member has had some direct experience with robotic surgery, here is a child-friendly resource: http://thekidshouldseethis.com/post/a-surgical-robot-delicately-stitches-a-grape-back-together. This is a video demonstration of robotic surgery on a grape.

Activity 4.4
Robot Arm

At the age of fourteen, Easton LaChappelle used Lego blocks, fishing wire, and a 3-D printer to invent a robotic arm. It was a significant improvement on existing technologies because it could be built at a fraction of the cost of prosthetic devices then on the market. This BBC video describes Easton's design process: www.bbc.com/future/story/20151026-a-teens-mind-controlled-arm-could-make-prosthetics-cheaper.

I recommend this video for educators as an inspirational example of the power of tinkering and creative exploration. The content and vocabulary are probably too advanced for most young children. For young children, it's hard to find developmentally appropriate print or video resources that describe the amazing robotic devices, such as prosthetic arms and legs, that have been invented to help people with disabilities. Many of the stories and videos mention the accidents or illnesses that caused limb loss or paralysis. Even a brief mention of this kind of accident or illness might be difficult for young children to take in.

And yet most young children have seen or heard about artificial arms or legs, as well as wheelchairs and other devices that help people live more active and productive lives. Some of the children in your classroom may have family members who need or use these kinds of devices. If the topic of robotic arms or legs seems relevant to the children in your class, or if a child asks about it, I have two recommendations.

First, this video describes an amazing project that allows children to design and make their own robotic limbs using components similar to Lego toys: http://thekidshouldseethis.com/post/a-prosthetic-system-that-lets-kids-make-their-own-lego-robot-limbs. Another way to approach the topic of assistive devices is through animals. There are many charming stories and videos about pets, especially dogs, who have lost the use of one or more limbs and have received some kind of assistive device, usually on wheels, to help them move around. Here's a great example: www.youtube.com/watch?v=4txTwafKlKc.

In the classroom, watch for a teachable moment related to assistive technologies. If a doll loses an arm or leg, for example, or a toy bird loses its wing, instead of throwing the toy away, ask the children if they can invent an artificial limb or

another type of device, real or pretend, to help the toy move or become whole again. Materials like Lego blocks, straws, craft sticks, cardboard, and masking tape may inspire children to design and build an exciting and innovative robotic or assistive device for a toy.

Activity 4.5
Yuck!

The conversations you have with the children about robots and the picture books about robots that you read to them will probably touch upon the idea that robots do things people don't like to do. For example, in Dan Yaccarino's book *If I Had a Robot*, the boy imagines a robot that will take over all his unwanted tasks, such as cleaning the house, feeding the dog, practicing piano, and even kissing his Aunt Louise.

In real life, robots actually do perform many tasks in industry and manufacturing that people don't like to do, such as moving or manipulating chemicals and other dangerous materials. In this activity, children gain some direct experience in the benefits and challenges of having robots do human work. As they do so, they can ponder the following big questions:

▶ How can robots help us?

▶ What jobs can robots do?

▶ How do we design and build robots that work?

For this activity, you will need the following materials:

- bin or water table

- washable household items or toys of various sizes and shapes, such as utensils, Lego blocks, coins, or cups

- large quantity of hair gel, pancake syrup, vegetable oil, or other sticky or goopy substance, enough to coat the bottom of the bin and the items in the bin

- toy robot arm, toy grabber, kitchen tongs, or ice tongs

Place the household items or toys in the bin and cover them with a thin layer of hair gel or other goopy substance. Say to the children, "Now we need to pick up these items. Would you like to pick them up with your fingers, or would you rather have a robot do it for you?"

Invite the children to use the robot arm, grabber, or tongs to pick up the items. As the children do this task, ask them open-ended questions that will help them identify the challenges of picking up small items, large items, smooth items, rough items, or bumpy items. Also, ask questions that help children evaluate the design and function of the robotic arm, grabber, or tongs:

▶ How does this tool work?

▶ Is this a good tool for this job? Why or why not?

▶ How could we make a robot that would do this job for us? What would the robot look like?

▶ What parts and pieces would the robot have?

▶ What materials would the robot be made of?

Invite children to draw a picture of a robot that would be good at picking up sticky things or slippery things.

Activity 4.6
Robot Car

The topic of self-driving cars has been at the top of tech and business news recently. According to *Fortune* magazine, today's five-year-old will grow up in a world where we will all routinely order an autonomous self-driving car using an app on our smartphones. The car will quickly pick us up and drop us off at our destination as we enjoy a stress-free, energy-efficient ride (Korosec 2016).

Currently there are only a few children's books in print that discuss the topic of self-driving cars. Certainly, as the technology becomes more widely used, more books will be written and published. For now, check out the following:

- *Self-Driving Cars* by Katie Marsico

- *Self-Driving Cars* by Christine Zuchora-Walske

In addition, Daimler, the parent company of automaker Mercedes-Benz, has published an e-book for children that introduces the concept of self-driving cars. It's titled *Where Do Cars Go at Night?* You can access the children's book free online using this link: http://issuu.com/moovellab/docs/151105_wdcgan_inhalt.

I would argue that the concept of self-driving cars is not at all strange to young children. When preschool children play with toy cars, usually the car itself is the main character in their pretend scenarios. Children rarely include the role of the driver in their pretend play with toy cars, unless the toy car is large and detailed enough to include a space for a toy driver to sit and a window or door that allows the child to place the driver in the car.

The characteristic of self-driving cars that might be most interesting and meaningful to young children is the way that self-driving cars can potentially eliminate or reduce traffic jams. When human-driven cars are stopped at a traffic light and the light turns green, the driver of the first car moves her car forward first, then the second car begins moving, and then the third. When a row of automated cars is stopped at a traffic light and the light turns green, the cars begin to move in synchronized fashion, kind of like a train. You might demonstrate this concept with children in an early childhood classroom by comparing a toy train with linked cars to individual toy cars. Or you could let this concept emerge during children's spontaneous play and then facilitate a conversation that helps children observe and understand how vehicles move when their movements are synchronized.

Another way to connect children's play and the concept of self-driving or robotic cars is to invite children to create a traffic jam with toy vehicles. Most children will welcome the opportunity to create a crazy mess of cars moving in all directions. Then challenge children to think of a way to solve that problem and keep the traffic jam from happening. Would children change how the roads are laid out? Would they change the way the roads come together? Would they change the traffic lights or signals? Would they change the cars' speed? These questions will help children analyze a complex problem, break it down into different ideas or variables, and brainstorm potential solutions.

As children do this activity, they can ponder the following big questions:

▸ Can a robot drive a car?

▸ How could you create a robot or a computer that could drive a car?

▸ Would a car driven by a robot look or work differently than a car driven by a person?

As a follow-up activity, I recommend the logic game Rush Hour. It engages children in the kinds of logical and computational thinking that parallel the programming of self-driving cars. It is recommended for ages eight years and up (www.thinkfun.com/products/rush-hour). Rush Hour Jr. is recommended for ages five years and up (www.thinkfun.com/products/rush-hour-jr). Rush Hour can also be played free online here: www.thinkfun.com/play-online/rush-hour.

Activity 4.7
Fast and Faster

Factories use robotic devices to help speed up the manufacturing process. Robots can often work faster and more efficiently than human beings. Here are three child-friendly videos that demonstrate how robots are used in industry:

- Lego factory robots: http://thekidshouldseethis.com/post/inside-the-lego-factory-the-robots-machines-that-make-lego

- ultrafast robots: http://thekidshouldseethis.com/post/two-ultra-fast-robots-pick-place-batteries-to-form-group-patterns

- robots decorating a cake: http://thekidshouldseethis.com/post/automated-cake-icing-and-decorating-machines

After watching one of these videos, children may enjoy the challenge of trying to accomplish a familiar task at top speed. Find a simple physical task, such as putting together a puzzle or placing pegs in a pegboard. Have children perform the task at a regular pace, and time them with a stopwatch or clock. Then have them do it again, speeding up as much as they can. Compare how long they took to do it the first time to how long it took them the second time. Then ask, "Did you make any mistakes when you tried to go faster? Did you drop anything or have trouble making things fit?" This experience will help inform children's understanding of the challenges and benefits of automating a task.

Activity 4.8
Robot Directions

Many young children have observed adults ask for and receive directions from a voice-activated GPS navigation system or smartphone while they are driving. This is another example of an electronic device that helps people.

In a small group, ask children if they have ever seen anyone ask for directions using a computer or a phone. If you have a tablet, smartphone, or other device available, demonstrate for the children how navigation apps work. Even if you are not driving in a car, you can still show the children how to ask for directions to a location and hear how the device tells you to navigate. For example, on an iPhone, you could ask Siri for directions to the closest grocery store or library. Invite the children to take turns asking for directions to landmarks they know.

Ask the children to describe the automated voice they hear when they use these devices. Does it sound like a real person? Why or why not?

Activity 4.9
Brave Robots

While the Transformer films and cartoons include conflict, suspense, and violence that are not suitable for young children, children of all ages seem to be familiar with Transformer characters and toys. Almost any discussion of robots among children over the age of two will inevitably include some reference to a Transformer. In case you are still in the dark about these creatures, Transformers are robotic creatures from another planet that can transform into other kinds of machines. For example, the Transformer hero and leader, Optimus Prime, is a broad-shouldered robot with the profile of a muscular superhero. Optimus Prime is able to transform into a souped-up semitrailer.

As part of your conversations with children about robots that help people, ask the children, "Can a robot be brave?" Some of the children may enthusiastically say yes and use Transformers as an example. This is a great opportunity to lead the children to a discussion about how robots and machines might help people in real life. Robots are frequently used in situations that would be dangerous for humans. Firefighting robots provide one great example:

- This article includes a photo of a robotic device that helps fight forest fires: http://wildfiretoday.com/2015/12/11/firefighting-robots.

- This video shows a snakelike, water-spraying robot that may someday be used by firefighters to put out fires: www.allonrobots.com/firefighting-robots.html.

- And here's a video of a wheeled robot called Quince. Quince goes into an area damaged by an earthquake to see if the area is safe: www.youtube.com/watch?v=taKbsFRNRT4.

Activity 4.10
Robot Friends

Many children's picture books about robots tell stories in which a robot character develops a friendship with a child. One example is *Robot, Go Bot!* by Dana Meachen Rau. In this story, a girl builds a robot out of spare parts. The girl and her robot play together happily until the robot grows tired of being bossed around. The robot frowns and looks very unhappy until the girl treats the robot with more kindness and lets the robot have a turn on a swing. The two characters in the story interact in the way two human friends would interact. The story is a sweet lesson in the golden rule: treat others the way you would like to be treated. The illustrations are colorful and the story is engaging, but be aware that *Robot, Go Bot!* could actually undermine children's understanding of the real relationship between people and robots. You may need to remind children that robots are programmable. We create commands using code, and the robots perform those commands.

And yet both children and adults enjoy personifying machines. Some of us name our cars and blow kisses to our coffee machines. We become fond of the tools that help us lead happy and productive lives. There's nothing wrong with thinking of robots as our friends, especially when they look and move like people. In fact, here's an example of a robot that the developers claim is so friendly, helpful, and intelligent that it will become part of your family: www.jibo.com. The Jibo robot can take family photos and videos, read and send messages, turn on your lights and appliances, order your dinner, and even read you a bedtime story.

Activity 4.11
Sensors—How Robots See

The educational robots introduced in chapter 3, such as Bee-Bot and Cubetto, do not have sensors. But as children begin to learn more about and gain more experience with robotic devices, they may become aware that some robots can respond to their environment. Sensors allow robots to see lights and colors, to hear sounds and voices, and to detect motion. Some robots can even smell and taste.

In the world of educational robots, an example of a robot with a sensor is the tiny Ozobot (http://ozobot.com). The Ozobot can follow a line of color drawn on a piece of paper. The Ozobot rolls across the page as its color sensors read the code represented by the pattern of colors.

Lego Mindstorms EV3 robots also have light and color sensors that allow them to follow a line. EV3 kits are commonly used in First Lego League clubs and after-school enrichment programs. If your conversations with children lead to a discussion of how robots see or hear, you can introduce them to the world of Lego robots by inviting an older child from a local Lego club to visit your classroom or by watching one of these videos:

- a video of Segway-style robotic devices made with Lego robotic parts and sensors: www.youtube.com/watch?v=5fNYDkjgO4M

- a video demonstrating the use of the color sensor in Lego EV3 robotic kits: www.youtube.com/watch?v=8wzXIhEF7V4

- a video of a robotics competition hosted at University of Nevada: www.youtube.com/watch?v=yTRy6P1SbjA

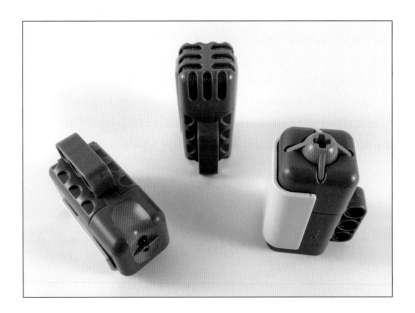

Activity 4.12
Flying Robots

The practical uses of flying robots are described in the nonfiction picture book *Weather Robots* by Christine Zuchora-Walske. You could use the photos and ideas in this book to initiate a conversation about how robots help people understand and predict the weather. If your classroom has a morning ritual that includes talking about the weather, that would be a good time to connect what people need to know and what robots can do.

For example, ask the children to make a weather prediction: "Do you think it will rain today? Why or why not?" Then you might wonder out loud, "I wish I could fly into the clouds and look to see if rain is coming." Some children may laugh, but some might find that idea fascinating. Ask the children, "Would you like to fly into a rain cloud or a storm cloud? Why or why not?" If any of the children recognize that flying into a storm might be dangerous, that's a good opportunity for making the robot connection. Ask, "What about a robot? Could we send a robot into a storm cloud?" At this point, it might be helpful to use photos from a nonfiction book like *Weather Robots* to help children imagine how a flying robot might work.

Children may also enjoy viewing the beauty and complexity of the flying robot featured in this video: http://thekidshouldseethis.com/post/8755755598.

Activity 4.13
What Is a Drone?

Drones are so commonly used now by hobbyists and professional photographers that many young children have heard the term "drone" and have seen drones in action. A drone is a remote-controlled flying device. It has no pilot or passenger.

Here are two fascinating child-friendly examples of drones:

- tiny drones with four propellers called nano quadrotors: http://thekidshouldseethis.com/post/16922370178

- a flying robot orchestra: http://thekidshouldseethis.com /post/84441470252

Activity 4.14
Swimming Robots

Chapter 2 of this book recommends Hexbugs for classroom use as an example of bio-inspired robots. The same company that makes Hexbugs also makes swimming robots called AquaBots. The Hexbug AquaBots come in several different varieties. The one with the simplest design, the basic AquaBot single fish, provides a great example of the use of sensors (www.hexbug.com/aquabot/hexbug-aquabot -8482-single.html).

When you drop this robotic fish into a bathtub or fish tank, it begins to swim. This is because the AquaBot has two pressure sensors, one on each side of its body. When there is equal pressure on both sides, the fish's tail begins to move.

This toy inspires an exciting example of inquiry-based learning. When you don't tell children about the sensors or explain how the sensors work, you challenge and inspire them to observe and test until they can begin to develop their own ideas about how the fish knows it's in the water. At first, most of us will guess that it's the water itself that triggers the movement, that the fish knows when it is wet. Some children, however, may be able to figure out on their own that there are pressure sensors on the sides of the fish, through careful observation and testing.

As an extension activity, children may enjoy testing their own "sensors." Have children touch the contents of three bowls with three different textures or sensations. I suggest one filled with water, just like the environment of the AquaBot; one bowl filled with something wet but somewhat solid like soggy noodles or gelatin; and one filled with a dry and loose substance like rice or sand. Have the children close their eyes and dip their hands in each of the substances. Ask them to say "Now!" when they can feel the substance on both sides of their hand. Ask, "How did you know your hand was in the water (or other substance)? What did it feel like? Could you feel any pressure on your skin? Can you imagine what it might feel like to be the AquaBot in the water? Can you imagine the gentle pressure it feels on its sensors?"

Children may also enjoy viewing videos of more complex examples of swimming robots:

- air penguin: www.youtube.com/watch?v=jPGgl5VH5go

- robotic jellyfish: www.youtube.com/watch?v=N-O8-N71Qcw

Activity 4.15
Robots in Space

If children's pretend play and conversations demonstrate an interest in space travel, you can probably find several nonfiction children's books about the use of robots for space exploration at your local library, such as these two:

- *Robots in Space* by Nancy Furstinger

- *Robots in Space* by Kathryn Clay

The example that young children usually find most interesting is the Mars rover. Here are a few videos you might share with children:

- "Testing with a Martian Dune Buggy": http://thekidshouldseethis.com /post/27554318150

- "Mars Science Laboratory (Curiosity Rover) Mission Animation": http://thekidshouldseethis.com/post/8395436365

- "Testing a Space Rover under Alaskan Ice": http://thekidshouldseethis.com /post/testing-a-space-rover-under-alaskan-ice

Activity 4.16
Robot Wishes

Invite children to make robot wishes. This activity can help children make meaningful connections between what they are learning about robots and how their ideas and inventions might help change the world in the future.

A robot wish is the seed of an idea that might someday turn into an invention. Start a sentence that begins "I wish I had a robot that could . . ." and invite the children to finish the sentence. Write down children's ideas on a poster or in a book.

When children encounter a challenge or frustration, offer a "robot wish" as a way to brainstorm solutions. For example, if a child drops a basket of crackers and creates a mess on the floor, the child might wish for a robot to help sweep the floor.

Sometimes robot wishes can spark real and immediate solutions. Robot wishes can also help us recognize that sometimes we can solve our problems on our own and that, in fact, sometimes it's even better to offer comfort and assistance to one another without a robot's help.

5

How Can We Learn More about Robots?

Robotics and Computer Science in Elementary School and Beyond

The resources and activities in this chapter provide a pathway for continuing robotics, computer science, and STEM learning beyond early childhood. For young children with advanced abilities and interests in computer science and robotics, this information will help teachers and families differentiate and provide challenges beyond a more typical early childhood level. These resources and activities may also be valuable to educators who create and implement after-school and enrichment programs for children in the primary grades. Additionally, the information may be helpful to guide professional development tools for teachers who are interested in advancing their own knowledge and expertise in STEM and computer science.

Activity 5.1
Scratch Animation

Scratch is a free visual programming language developed for educational use by computer scientists at the Massachusetts Institute of Technology more than a decade ago. The ScratchJr app described in chapter 3 was more recently designed as a tool for young children. However, the original Scratch tools, curriculum, and online community are still widely used to teach and develop coding skills for children starting around age eight. The Scratch website (https://scratch.mit.edu) also offers extensive resources for teachers and families.

Activity 5.2
Hopscotch

Hopscotch is a free drag-and-drop programming app that allows children to create their own animated stories and games (www.gethopscotch.com). Hopscotch is similar to ScratchJr but is a bit more challenging. Hopscotch tools and tutorials are focused more on creating games, while ScratchJr is more about creating and telling stories.

Activity 5.3
Digital Game Design

Many children are inspired to learn how to code because they enjoy playing digital games and would like to create their own. Digital gaming is an exciting and popular area of exploration for older children. Everywhere you look, new apps and tools are available to teach children how to create their own digital games. The options can be overwhelming. I recommend Blockly Games as an introductory tool, because it provides a quick sample of different kinds of games and coding tasks. I also recommend Gamestar Mechanic:

- Blockly Games (https://blockly-games.appspot.com): To explore the different kinds of games that can be played and created using code, Google created the website Blockly Games.

- Gamestar Mechanic (https://gamestarmechanic.com): Gamestar Mechanic is a web-based digital game creator for use by schools or individuals. The online design activities teach children the fundamentals of game design. Recently PBS Kids teamed up with Gamestar Mechanic to create a version for younger children called Gamestar Mechanic Jr, available online at http://pbskids.org /gamestarmechanicjr.

Activity 5.4
Hour of Code

HOUR OF CODE

Hour of Code is an initiative created by a collaborative of tech giants, including Facebook, Apple, and Microsoft. Its goal is to inspire students of all backgrounds to learn how to code and to develop skills and expertise in computer science. This initiative has reached over 100 million students in more than 180 countries.

The official global Hour of Code takes place annually in early December, but an amazing variety of Hour of Code tutorials are available online all year long (https://code.org/learn). While the Star Wars, Minecraft, and Frozen animated tutorials were clearly created for children, adults are encouraged to try an Hour of Code tutorial too. If you have no background in computer science or feel intimidated by the swift pace of tech innovation, completing an Hour of Code tutorial can help you feel more confident about learning and understanding coding concepts. You may be surprised at how easy and fun coding can be.

Hour of Code has many educational partners, and the list keeps growing. One of the most prominent partners is Khan Academy, an excellent source of free online courses and STEM resources (www.khanacademy.org/hourofcode).

Other Hour of Code partner tutorials provide fun, free samples of new coding apps, such as the following:

- CodeMonkey
- CS First
- The Foos
- Lightbot

- Run Marco!
- Scratch
- Tynker

Activity 5.5
Code.org Code Studio

Code.org, the host site of Hour of Code, also provides an exceptional series of free coding exercises and games called Code Studio (https://studio.code.org) that teach students the basics of programming. The core offerings include four Computer Science Fundamentals courses for students, starting at age four.

More recent additions to Code Studio include accelerated courses for children ages ten to eighteen and a JavaScript App Lab for ages thirteen and older.

Activity 5.6
Hello Ruby

Hello Ruby is both a children's book by Linda Liukas and a website (www.helloruby .com). Ruby's story and activities teach children strategies for computational thinking, such as how to break down a big problem into smaller tasks.

Activity 5.7
Web Design and App Invention

As children develop more advanced coding skills, they may become interested in creating a website or an app. Khan Academy provides free online computer science courses. The introductory web design courses teach students hypertext markup language (HTML), the programming language used to create web pages (www .khanacademy.org/computing/computer-programming/html-css). Code Academy is another free site with similar offerings (www.codecademy.com/courses/web -beginner-en-HZA3b/0/1). For app design, MIT App Inventor is an app creation tool for beginning programmers. MIT App Inventor does not require an understanding of HTML. Programmers simply drag and drop blocks using a graphic interface (http://appinventor.mit.edu/explore).

Activity 5.8
Lego WeDo, EV3, and VEX

For a long time, Lego robotics kits were pretty much the only option for kids who wanted to learn how to build and code a robot. Lego Mindstorms robotics kits were first introduced around 2000. There have been several versions and updates over the years. Lego EV3 kits are the current version of Mindstorms (www.lego.com /en-us/mindstorms/about-ev3). Lego WeDo kits are a simpler version of Mindstorms (https://education.lego.com/en-us/elementary/shop/wedo-2). EV3 is considered appropriate for middle school students, and WeDo for elementary school students. Both WeDo and EV3 kits come with the hardware to build a variety of robots, including the corresponding software to download to a laptop or tablet.

Lego now faces competition from many different robotics kits and systems marketed to both schools and families. For example, Innovation First International, the corporation that manufactures and sells Hexbug toys, also markets VEX EDR, a robotics design platform, and kits that are comparable to Lego Mindstorms (www .vexrobotics.com). The February/March 2017 issue of *Make:* magazine includes a helpful guide to the growing field of robot kits (see "Which Robotics Kit Is Right for You?" Volume 55): http://makezine.com/tag/make55.

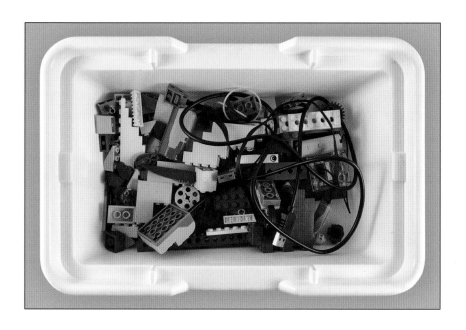

Activity 5.9
First Lego League

In most US schools, robotics and computer science are not yet part of the core curriculum. When elementary, middle, and high school students are exposed to robotics, it's often in the form of a robotics club that meets after school. First Lego League is an international network of robotics teams led by volunteer coaches (www.firstlegoleague.org). The league provides a structure for meets where teams compete against one another to design and code robots in response to specific challenges and specifications.

Activity 5.10
Makerspaces

A makerspace is a place where inventors and tinkerers can explore new ideas using many different kinds of open-ended materials. The maker movement began among adults who enjoyed building electronic gadgets as a hobby. The innovative maker spirit and the opportunities for design thinking and STEM learning in makerspaces has created an interest in bringing the maker experience to younger and younger students.

Many of the activities presented in this book are already aligned with a maker philosophy. For more information about makerspaces and how to integrate maker ideas into your classroom, check out these essential maker resources.

Books

- *The Art of Tinkering: Meet 150+ Makers Working at the Intersection of Art, Science, and Technology* by Karen Wilkinson and Mike Petrich

- *Design, Make, Play: Growing the Next Generation of STEM Innovators* edited by Margaret Honey and David E. Kanter

- *Invent to Learn: Making, Tinkering, and Engineering in the Classroom* by Sylvia Libow Martinez and Gary S. Stager

- *Make Space: How to Set the Stage for Creative Collaboration* by Scott Doorley and Scott Witthoft

Article

- "Making with Young Children: An Introduction" (www.naeyc.org/tyc /making-young-learners-intro)

Websites

- Make: (http://makezine.com)

- Instructables (www.instructables.com)

- Thinkers & Tinkers (http://hernbergm.wix.com/maker-movement)

Activity 5.11
Ready, Set, Design

Ready, Set, Design is a fun and easy group activity that introduces and illustrates design thinking. The activity could be implemented with adults as well as with children as young as first or second grade. This technique could be adapted easily for younger children. I recommend it as a team-building activity with teachers.

The activity is fairly simple. You divide participants into small groups and give each group a paper bag filled with a small amount of three different kinds of construction materials:

- fastener items (such as rubber bands or paper clips)

- surface items (such as coffee filters or index cards)

- structure items (such as straw or foil)

You also give each team a challenge written on an index card, such as "Make something that carries water" or "Make something that helps people stay healthy." The group has a short period of time to work. Participants must quickly brainstorm and create a prototype for some kind of invention that will meet the challenge.

Ready, Set, Design was created by the Cooper Hewitt, Smithsonian Design Museum to teach design thinking. You can learn about this technique here: www.cooperhewitt.org/2011/09/09/ready-set-design. You can find the full instructions here: http://cdn.cooperhewitt.org/2011/09/02/Ready%20Set%20Design%20vX.pdf.

Activity 5.12
Interview a Robot Expert

Children who develop a particular interest in robotics and computer science benefit from the opportunity to meet and talk with role models who are working in this field. If you live near a college or university with an engineering program, look on the school's website for a listing of the robotics faculty. Most robotics engineers would be thrilled to talk with children about their work. Here's an example of an online talk with Dr. Michael Peshkin, a robotics professor at Northwestern University: www.youtube.com/watch?v=Rz8HwWCJFVw&feature=youtu.be.

Activity 5.13
Visit a Science Museum

Science museums are fantastic resources for families and educators. To find a science museum near you, use this tool provided by the Association of Science-Technology Centers: www.astc.org/about-astc/about-science-centers/find-a-science-center.

Here are a few of my favorite science museums:

- New York Hall of Science in Queens, New York City (http://nysci.org)

- Museum of Science and Industry in Chicago, Illinois (www.msichicago.org)

- Carnegie Science Center in Pittsburgh, Pennsylvania (www.carnegiesciencecenter.org)

Even if you don't live near a science museum or science center, the websites for these organizations often provide amazing free STEM resources and lesson plans for educators.

Activity 5.14
Visit a Robotics Lab

Many major universities have robotics labs where faculty and students build robots and conduct research. Some of these are occasionally open to the public. Here are two examples of robotics labs:

- Stanford Robotics Lab (http://cs.stanford.edu/groups/manips)

- Robotics at UT Austin (https://robotics.utexas.edu)

If you can't visit a robotics lab in person, the website for the MIT Computer Science and Artificial Intelligence Laboratory provides a virtual tour: www.csail.mit.edu/about/tour/virtual/Robotics_Lab.

Activity 5.15
Follow a Robot Blog

For inspiration and information, follow a robotics group or blog online. Here are some notable examples:

- Classroom Robotics (http://classroomrobotics.blogspot.com)

- Popular Science: Robotics (www.popsci.com/find/robotics)

- Robohub (http://robohub.org)

Activity 5.16
Girls in STEM

Unfortunately, girls are significantly underrepresented in STEM classrooms. According to the US Department of Education, high school boys are much more likely than girls are to enroll in challenging STEM courses such as calculus, statistics, and physics (US DOE 2012). In college, young women are also a minority in STEM majors. And although women represent 48 percent of the total workforce after college, more than 75 percent of all STEM jobs are still held by men (Beede et al. 2011). If we want to encourage girls to pursue STEM studies and careers, we need to start early, before they encounter obstacles or bias that might make them turn away from challenging learning opportunities. As early childhood educators, we need to be aware that sometimes girls need a little extra encouragement to visit the block corner or build a robot.

Here are two resources that can help you encourage girls in STEM pursuits:

- Girls Who Code (https://girlswhocode.com) is a nonprofit organization dedicated to closing the gender gap in technology. It operates coding clubs and summer camps all over the United States.

- "Girls and Robotics" (www.edutopia.org/blog/girls-and-robotics-mary-beth -hertz) is an article that encourages educators to help girls become involved in robotics.

Recommended Resources

✿ STEM Resources

Erikson TEC Center
Resources for early childhood educators to help strengthen
children's digital literacy
https://teccenter.erikson.edu

Fred Rogers Center
Resources on early learning and children's media
www.fredrogerscenter.org

Joan Ganz Cooney Center
Research center that focuses on media technology and its
impact on children's learning in a digital age
www.joanganzcooneycenter.org

National Association for the Education of Young Children Science, Technology, Engineering, and Math Resources for Early Childhood
STEM resources for educators and families
www.naeyc.org/STEM

National Science Teachers Association
Resources for science teachers at all grade levels
www.nsta.org

✿ Robotics Resources

Carnegie Mellon Robotics Academy
Research and resources for robotics teachers
www.education.rec.ri.cmu.edu/content/lego

Early Childhood Robotics Network
A site for educators that was founded by the DevTech Research Group
at Tufts University
http://tkroboticsnetwork.ning.com

NASA Robotics Alliance Project

Robotics news and resources from the National Aeronautics and Space Administration

https://robotics.nasa.gov

✿ Coding Resources

Code.org

Nonprofit collaborative providing extensive computer science resources

https://code.org

Common Sense Education

Resources for teachers such as app reviews and teaching strategies

www.commonsense.org/education

K–12 Computer Science Framework

Guiding practices and concepts, including a chapter specific to early childhood education

https://k12cs.org

✿ Resources for Families

Common Sense Media

Media reviews and resources for families

www.commonsensemedia.org

Raising Digital Natives

Resources for parents from Devorah Heitner, author of *Screenwise*

www.raisingdigitalnatives.com

✿ Recommended Robotic Devices and Kits

Bee-Bot

www.bee-bot.us

Primo Cubetto

www.redleafpress.org/Cubetto-Playset-Coding-Robot-P1892.aspx

Code-a-Pillar

http://fisher-price.mattel.com/shop/en-us/fp/think-learn-code-a-pillar-dkt39

Hexbugs

www.hexbug.com

Robot Turtles Board Game

www.robotturtles.com

Snap Circuits

www.snapcircuits.net

Lego WeDo

(recommended in Section 5 for older children)
https://education.lego.com/en-us/shop/wedo%202

⚙ Picture Books Used in Activities

Car Wash by Sandra Steen and Susan Steen

Daisy's Wild Ride by Bob Graham

If I Had a Robot by Dan Yaccarino

If I Had a Robot Dog by Andrea Baruffi

Me and My Robot by Tracey West

The Most Magnificent Thing by Ashley Spires

Robot Rumpus by Sean Taylor

Robots at Home by Christine Zuchora-Walske

Rosie Revere, Engineer by Andrea Beaty

Weather Robots by Christine Zuchora-Walske

*See also the list of recommended robot picture books on page 29.

Glossary of Key Terms

algorithm: a set of step-by-step instructions for completing a task

app: a type of software for a mobile device, such as a tablet or smartphone

calibration: the process of adjusting for precise standardization of measurement; a robot may be calibrated to travel a certain distance with each command

code: a system of symbols for communication; in computer science, a code is a set of instructions written in a programming language

computational thinking: the ability to organize a problem so that it can be represented by logical steps

conditions or conditionals: a feature of a programming language that directs the computer to follow the coded instructions based on whether certain criteria are met; conditions may be described using the words "if" and "then"

dimension: in mathematics, dimension is the measurement in one direction; two-dimensional or 2-D objects, which are flat, can be measured in two directions, and three-dimensional or 3-D objects, which are solid, can be measured in three directions

directionality: in the context of spatial reasoning, directionality is the relationship between the position of an object and the various directions of potential travel or movement, such as right, left, forward, or back

drag and drop: a method for using an app or playing a digital game that allows the user to manipulate objects or text using a mouse or, in the case of a touch screen, a finger

function: in computer programming, a procedure or routine that has been created and stored for later use

grid: a network of uniformly placed horizontal and vertical lines

hardware: the physical components of a computer or robot

interface: the place where two systems meet and communicate, such as the interface between people and computers; in computer programming, the word "interface" is often used to generally describe the overall experience of the user in regards to a specific application, device, or platform

Internet: the global collection of connected computer networks

loop: a programming structure that repeats a sequence of instructions

platform: in computer science, the operating system or architecture that makes the applications available to the user

program: a set of instructions that a computer or robot uses to complete a task; programming refers to the process of creating a program

sequence: a particular order of events or things, one following another

software: programs that run on a computer or computing system

spatial reasoning: a category of thinking skills related to how objects are positioned or move in three dimensions; the term "spatial intelligence" refers to the ability to understand spatial relationships and perform spatial reasoning tasks

symbol: an image, mark, or character that represents an object, process, or idea

synchronization: the operation and coordination of two or more objects or processes at the same time

troubleshooting or debugging: a systematic process of solving a problem or correcting an error

visual programming: any programming language that allows the user to create programs by manipulating program elements graphically; may also be called block programming

References

Beaty, Andrea. 2013. *Rosie Revere, Engineer*. New York: Abrams.

Beede, David, Tiffany Julian, David Langdon, George McKittrick, Beethika Khan, and Mark Doms. 2011. *Women in STEM: A Gender Gap to Innovation: Executive Summary*. Washington, DC: Economics and Statistics Administration, US Department of Commerce. ESA Issue Brief #04-11. www.esa.doc.gov/sites /default/files/womeninstemagaptoinnovation8311.pdf.

Bers, Marina Umaschi. 2008. *Blocks to Robots: Learning with Technology in the Early Childhood Classroom*. New York: Teachers College Press.

Bers, Marina Umaschi, and Michael S. Horn. 2010. "Tangible Programming in Early Childhood: Revisiting Developmental Assumptions through New Technologies." In *High-Tech Tots: Childhood in a Digital World*, edited by Ilene R. Berson and Michael J. Berson, 49–69. Charlotte, NC: Information Age Publishing.

Blackwell, C. K. 2015. "iPads in Kindergarten: The Effect of Tablet Computers on Young Children's Academic Achievement." Paper presented at the 65th Annual Conference of the International Communication Association, San Juan, PR, May.

Brosterman, Norman. 1997. *Inventing Kindergarten*. New York: Harry N. Abrams.

Brown, Margaret Wise. 1999. *The Important Book*. New York: HarperCollins.

Ceppi, Giulio, Graziano Delrio, Elena Giacopini, et al. 2014. *Bikes . . . Lots!* Reggio Emilia, Italy: Reggio Children.

Chao, Grace. 2015. "What Is Design Thinking?" *Stanford Daily*, May 15. www.stanforddaily.com/what-is-design-thinking.

Common Sense. 2017. "Our Mission." Common Sense Media. Accessed January 19. www.commonsensemedia.org/about-us/our-mission.

CPS (Chicago Public Schools). 2016. "New CPS Computer Science Graduation Requirement to Prepare Students for Jobs of the Future." http://cps.edu/News /Press_releases/Pages/PR2_02_24_2016.aspx.

EIE (Engineering Is Elementary). 2017. "The Engineering Design Process." Accessed January 13. www.eie.org/eie-curriculum/engineering-design-process.

Forman, George. 2012. "The Use of Digital Media in Reggio Emilia." In *The Hundred Languages of Children: The Reggio Emilia Experience in Transformation,* 3rd ed., edited by Carolyn Edwards, Lella Gandini, and George Forman, 343–56. Santa Barbara, CA: Praeger.

Google Inc. and Gallup Inc., 2016. *Trends in the State of Computer Science in U.S. K-12 Schools*. Accessed May 15, 2017. http://services.google.com/fh/files/misc /trends-in-the-state-of-computer-science-report.pdf.

Gopnik, Alison. 2016. "What Babies Know about Physics and Foreign Languages." *New York Times*, July 30. http://nyti.ms/2aCYCAW.

Hord, Mike. 2017. "PCB Basics." Sparkfun. Accessed January 12. https://learn .sparkfun.com/tutorials/pcb-basics.

Idaho Public Television. 2014. "Simple Machines: Facts." Science Trek. Accessed January 21. http://idahoptv.org/sciencetrek/topics/simple_machines/facts.cfm.

Joan Ganz Cooney Center. 2017. "Initiatives." Accessed January 19. www.joanganzcooneycenter.org/initiatives.

Korosec, Kirsten. 2016. "There's Now a Children's Book about Self-Driving Cars." *Fortune*, October 18. http://fortune.com/2016/10/18/children-self-driving-cars.

Kris, Deborah Farmer. 2015. "Steps to Help Foster a Preschooler's Spatial Reasoning Skills." KQED Mind/Shift. https://ww2.kqed.org/mindshift/2015/12/16 /steps-to-help-foster-a-preschoolers-spatial-reasoning-skills.

K12CSF (K–12 Computer Science Framework). 2016. *K–12 Computer Science Framework*. https://k12cs.org/wp-content/uploads/2016/09/K–12-Computer-Science -Framework.pdf.

LA Tech STEP. 2007. "What Is a Gear?" Louisiana Tech University. www.latech.edu /latechstep/p/pf/gi.pdf.

NAEYC and FRC (National Association for the Education of Young Children and Fred Rogers Center for Early Learning and Children's Media at Saint Vincent College). 2012. *Technology and Interactive Media as Tools in Early Childhood Programs Serving Children from Birth through Age 8*. www.naeyc.org/files/naeyc /file/positions/PS_technology_WEB2.pdf.

NMSI (National Math and Science Initiative). 2017. "Why STEM Education Matters." Accessed January 3. https://www.nms.org/Portals/0/Docs/Why%20Stem %20Education%20Matters.pdf.

Papert, Seymour. 1980. *Mindstorms: Children, Computers, and Powerful Ideas*. New York: Basic Books.

ScratchEd. 2017. "Computational Thinking." Accessed January 5. http://scratched
.gse.harvard.edu/ct/files/CT_Definitions.pdf.

Sessions, Larry. 2016. "Seeing Things That Aren't There." EarthSky. http://earthsky
.org/human-world/seeing-things-that-arent-there.

Slobodkina, Esphyr. 1987. *Caps for Sale: The Tale of a Peddler, Some Monkeys, and
Their Monkey Business*. New York: HarperCollins.

UK Department for Education. 2013. "National Curriculum in England: Computing
Programmes of Study." www.gov.uk/government/publications/national
-curriculum-in-england-computing-programmes-of-study/national
-curriculum-in-england-computing-programmes-of-study.

US DOE (US Department of Education). 2012. "Gender Equity in Education:
A Data Snapshot." Office for Civil Rights. www2.ed.gov/about/offices/list/ocr
/docs/gender-equity-in-education.pdf.

West, Tracey. 2003. *Me and My Robot*. New York: Penguin Young Readers.